Workstyles to Fit Your Lifestyle

EVERYONE'S GUIDE TO TEMPORARY EMPLOYMENT

John Fanning
Rosemary Maniscalco

PRENTICE HALL
Englewood Cliffs, New Jersey 07632

Prentice-Hall International (UK) Limited, *London*
Prentice-Hall of Australia Pty. Limited, *Sydney*
Prentice-Hall Canada, Inc., *Toronto*
Prentice-Hall Hispanoamericana, S.A., *Mexico*
Prentice-Hall of India Private Limited, *New Delhi*
Prentice-Hall of Japan, Inc., *Tokyo*
Simon & Schuster Asia Pte. Ltd., *Singapore*
Editora Prentice-Hall do Brasil, Ltda., *Rio de Janeiro*

© 1993 *by*
John Fanning and Rosemary Maniscalco

10 9 8 7 6 5 4 3 2 1

Library of Congress Cataloging-in-Publication Data

Fanning, John.
    Workstyles to fit your lifestyle : everyone's guide to temporary
employment / by John Fanning and Rosemary Maniscalco.
        p.   cm.
    Includes index.
    ISBN 0-13-015728-7
    1. Temporary employment.   I. Maniscalco, Rosemary.
    II. Title.
HD5854.F36   1993
650.14—dc20   93-15548
                                                                    CIP

ISBN 0-13-015728-7

PRENTICE HALL
Career and Personal Development
Englewood Cliffs, NJ 07632

Simon & Schuster, A Paramount Communications Company

Printed in the United States of America

Acknowledgments

To Gene Busnar, whose collaboration on this book made it possible as well as pleasurable.

To the wind beneath our wings, Linda Annicelli, Uniforce Services' Director of Communications, who shores up our ship and always makes certain that we have our best foot forward.

To Jeff Herman, our literary agent, for bringing us to the right place at the right time with the right people and for his continuing advice and support.

Introduction

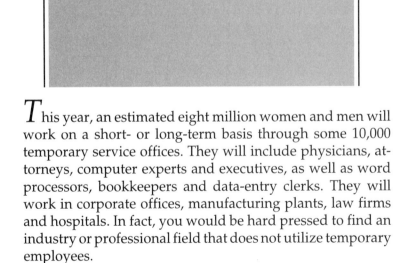

T his year, an estimated eight million women and men will work on a short- or long-term basis through some 10,000 temporary service offices. They will include physicians, attorneys, computer experts and executives, as well as word processors, bookkeepers and data-entry clerks. They will work in corporate offices, manufacturing plants, law firms and hospitals. In fact, you would be hard pressed to find an industry or professional field that does not utilize temporary employees.

The use of temporary staffers to fill positions has nearly doubled over the past ten years, and this trend is expected to continue through the 1990's. Traditionally, temporary employees were used in clerical fields to fill in for workers who were ill or on vacation. Today, temporaries can be found in almost every job category, filling a wide range of needs. In fact, temporary services have emerged as one of America's fastest-growing service businesses. Here's why: In today's competitive business climate, corporations require greater flexibility in addressing shifting economic and market conditions. By working closely with an experienced temporary service, companies can protect their profit margins by addressing their variable personnel needs. At the same time, recruitment, hiring and benefits costs are greatly reduced.

The growing demand for skilled temporaries is due, in great part, to the increase in office automation and other technological advances. Today's businesses need people who are educated and computer literate. In addition to a broad array of office jobs, temporary services are filling this need by providing a wide variety of training and cross-training opportunities.

It is fortuitous that the explosion in business's demand for temps is matched by the workstyle and lifestyle needs of so many people. The benefits of working as a temporary include:

1. Lifestyle flexibility that leaves more time for leisure and creative activities

2. The opportunity to sample a variety of work environments

3. Showcasing one's skills for possible permanent employment

4. The ability to hit the ground running when traveling or moving to a new city

5. A way to achieve a healthy balance between career and family

6. Workstyle flexibility that can be tailored to the needs of:

- Working mothers in two-income families
- People between jobs
- Empty nesters
- "1099" independent contractors
- Students
- Recent college graduates
- Retirees and early retirees
- Moonlighters
- Performing and creative artists
- Free spirits
- Career temps

In addition to the above advantages, the compensation, training opportunities and benefits in some areas of temporary employment have become sufficiently competitive that approximately one-third of all temps decide to pursue this workstyle as a career. Thousands more are using temping as a stepping stone to permanent, full-time jobs. According to the National Association of Temporary Services (NATS), 54 percent of all temporary employees are eventually offered permanent positions. This aspect of temporary employment is particularly important to recent college graduates and people out of work.

Our decision to write *Workstyles to Fit Your Lifestyle* was driven by a desire to fill a need. As leaders of one of America's larger temporary services, we have long been well aware of the flexible career options temping provides. At the same time, we were unable to find a book that showed people how to take advantage of the opportunities now available in the temporary employment industry.

Workstyles to Fit Your Lifestyle fills that gap by providing all the tools and information you need to earn money temping, while satisfying your short- and long-term career and lifestyle objectives. The chapters are equally useful whether you are considering temping as a short- or long-term career alternative—either now or sometime in the future.

In order to give you a broad perspective, we have supplemented our collective personal and professional experience with insights and anecdotes from a large cross-section of Uniforce licensees, temporary employees and corporate clients. We have also included a variety of checklists, interview tips and self-evaluation materials throughout the chapters to give you everything you need to:

- Realistically assess your marketable skills
- Select a service that can best address your requirements
- Maximize earnings
- Build in such perks as health benefits and vacations
- Formulate a personalized temporary employment game plan

The chapters are designed to help you customize the information to suit your unique needs. Sample interview questions and skill-assessment tests are included to help you prepare for interviews and job assignments. Firsthand anecdotes and practical advice will help you navigate unexpected or difficult situations. Time management, financial planning and other self-evaluation tools will aid you in realizing your workstyle and lifestyle objectives.

Our mission in writing this book is to give you a good understanding of the opportunities in temporary employment, an assessment of how well suited you are to take advantage of these opportunities and a personalized temporary employment game plan. We look forward to working with you.

John Fanning
Chief Executive Officer, Uniforce Services, Inc.

Rosemary Maniscalco
Chief Operating Officer, Uniforce Services, Inc.

Contents

▌ CHAPTER TWO:
Is Temporary Employment Right for You?   *15*

▌ CHAPTER THREE:
Taking Advantage of Expanding Opportunities in Today's and Tomorrow's Temporary Job Market   *35*

xi

▌▌ CHAPTER FOUR:
Working with a Temporary-Employment Service   61

▌▌ CHAPTER FIVE:
Congratulations, You're on Your Way!   95

█ CHAPTER SIX:
*Maximizing Your Money-Making
Potential*   115

▌ CHAPTER NINE:
Crisis and Transitional Temping: Money and Psychic Income When You Need It Most 183

▌ CHAPTER TEN:
Create Your Personalized Temporary Employment Game Plan 211

1

Temporary Services: The Field That's Always Hiring

"*A*merica's work force is changing. People don't want to work in one place anymore. Workers craving good jobs with flexible hours are turning to temporary services to help them find the perfect arrangement."[1]

Do one or more of the following statements describe you?

- I prefer working only when it suits my needs and wants.
- I am between positions and need to have money coming in.

- I am a wife and mother who wants to supplement my family's income.

- I am a recent college graduate seeking an entry-level position in a competitive field.

- I've been laid off or fired from my job, and I'm having trouble finding work.

- I've recently moved to a new location and need to start generating income immediately.

- I am a retired person who wants to remain active and productive without sacrificing my pension or benefits.

- I've been out of the job market for a number of years and would like to ease my way back while updating my skills.

- I am a performing or creative artist who requires flexibility and extra income.

If you can identify with any of the above statements, the world of temporary employment offers you a workstyle that can be custom tailored to your lifestyle needs. Once the primary domain of fill-in secretaries and out-of-work people, temping is now a viable option for some eight million women and men annually and 1 million in any one week in virtually every industry and professional field.

Did you know that today the pay scale, benefits and training opportunities in some areas of temporary employment have reached the point where thousands of people choose to decline permanent positions in favor of career temping?

Temporary employment provides unmatched flexibility as well as a number of unique challenges and career opportunities. Is temporary employment a viable option for you? In order to help you make an informed decision, we are going to want to learn a good deal about you. But first, let us tell you a little about us and how we came to write this book.

We are the chief executive officer and chief operating officer of Uniforce Services—a nationally franchised, publicly held temporary employment service with offices throughout the United States. Our joint experience spans well over six decades in the personnel field. In recent years, we've come in contact with a growing number of men and women who are interested in learning more about temporary employment. We've often wished we could recommend a hands-on guide that would tell people everything they needed to navigate the changing currents of today's temporary employment industry. Since we've never been able to find such a book, we decided to write it ourselves.

We invite you to join us on a journey through the rapidly expanding world of temporary employment. Together we'll explore the ins and outs of temping. You'll learn why temporary employment has emerged as one of America's fastest growing industries. You'll find out about the various kinds of temp services available in your area and how to work with them. We'll show you how to use temping to maximize your potential—both financially and personally.

Our discussion begins with an overview of the temporary employment industry and an exploration of the basics of successful temping. In Chapter Two, we will examine whether temping is a desirable alternative for you. In subsequent chapters, the discussion will focus on such timely issues as:

- How temping can help you generate more income during tough economic times

- Why you may want to consider joining the growing number of men and women who are choosing to become career temps

- The most sought-after and highest-paying temp job skills

- When temping is the most practical way to secure a desirable permanent position

- Unusual workstyles in changing times

- Why temping is the best way for homemakers to enter or reenter the workplace

- Rewarding second-career opportunities for retired persons
- Why temping is ideally suited to our ever more mobile society
- The new breed of professional temps: physicians, attorneys, engineers, computer experts, controllers, production managers and executives of all types

The information in this book is designed to help you whether you're considering temping as an interim or long-term career option. The chapters are also useful for those of you who already have temping experience.

As you come to appreciate the opportunities in temporary employment, you will be able to assess how well suited you are to take advantage of these openings and devise a personalized temporary employment game plan. But first, we'd like to briefly answer three questions that are among the most frequently asked by people who are interested in learning more about the growing world of temporary employment:

■ *How the Temporary Employment Industry Operates*

Temporary-help firms are paid by businesses to find and screen qualified employees. The client company pays an hourly service charge for each employee placed. There is never a charge to the temporary employee. The service makes its profit by marking up the hourly wage it pays its employees.

Qualified temporary employees have the advantage of being able to work when they want at a competitive rate of pay, while avoiding the time and drudgery of job hunting. Depending on the service, temporary personnel may be offered opportunities for training, as well as vacations and other fringe benefits.

Temporary-help services recruit new employees through advertising, word of mouth—and by offering bonuses to current employees for bringing new temps into the company. Before new temps are sent out on an assignment, they are evaluated in terms of skills, personality, attitude and appearance. This screening is accomplished through appropriate skill evaluations and in-person interviews.

To enable the service to quickly locate the right person to fill a business's needs, prospective employees are also evaluated in terms of skill level, work experience and availability. Temporary employees are, in effect, working for the temporary service, not for the company to which they report. It is the temp service that hires, fires and withholds taxes and social security.

 ## People Who Are Best Suited to Temping

Today's temporary positions are proving to be outstanding choices for working mothers, empty nesters, moonlighters, retirees and others who want or need to work when they choose. Temping gives unemployed and displaced individuals a way to make contacts and pay their rent while looking for permanent work. It also provides an opportunity for students and recent college graduates to gain valuable experience while testing the waters at a number of companies.

Some of you may decide to use temping as a stepping stone to permanent positions that would have otherwise been inaccessible. Many others will join the ranks of career temps—those who want or need a more flexible lifestyle that allows more time for family and outside interests. As you will see, there are any number of workstyle options you can custom tailor to your particular lifestyle needs.

 ## Why over Nine Out of Ten Companies Use Temporary Personnel

Businesses have been using temporary employees for decades. But in the 1980's, the industry began growing in leaps and bounds. By the early 1990's, the temporary employment industry emerged as America's third fastest-growing service business. Let's look at the two major factors that have fueled the unparalleled growth of this industry:

1. *Using temporary help makes it easier for businesses to control hiring, benefits and administration costs, thus enabling them to protect their profit margins.*

More and more businesses are finding that the hourly rate charged by temp services is offset by the savings in recruitment costs, fringe benefits, severance pay, worker's compensation and unemployment insurance—all of which are handled by the temporary service.

A good temporary service helps increase its client companies' profitability by absorbing the costs involved in advertising for new personnel, interviewing and checking references. Temporary services in some instances will also make available medical and other fringe benefits. This makes it possible, in many cases, for companies to shield themselves from these escalating costs, not to mention the paperwork and human resources involved in their administration.

By working closely with a good temporary service, a company can analyze and plan for peak work load periods and special projects. This advance planning enables companies to retain a core of permanent personnel for normal work load periods, supplemented by temporary personnel during peak periods, thus significantly reducing costs.

Imagine the scenario if temporary services did not exist: Companies would have to hire a sufficiently large work force to carry them through peak periods. Then, when business tailed off, they would have two options: Either retain employees whose services were no longer required or fire people and then rehire new personnel for the next peak period.

Both of these alternatives are expensive in terms of time and dollars. A judicious use of temporary personnel helps protect companies against the high cost of turnover, thus enabling them to remain competitive.

2. *The demand for skilled personnel is expanding at a much faster rate than the available labor force.*

Census Bureau statistics indicate that the number of men and women between the ages of 18 and 24 is declining.[2] Since this is the time when most young people join the work force, corporate America finds itself faced with a shortage of entry-level employees in many fields. This scarcity has made recruitment more difficult—and more expensive. Filling that gap is just one of many ways temporary services help their corporate clients.

The automation of the office environment has created a need for personnel who can operate computerized equipment on a multitude of software packages. As we approach the twenty-first century, there will be an ever-increasing demand for men and women who are proficient in a broad range of technical and computer-based skills. This demand extends from entry-level data entry and word processing to computer operations personnel, systems and applications programmers, systems analysts, network specialists, local area network (LAN), data base analysts, computer assisted designers (CAD), technical writers and numerical control (NC) operators and programmers.

Temporary services have become adept at satisfying corporate America's growing need for employees with these and other highly specialized skills. In order to fill their corporate clients' requirements for qualified employees, growth-oriented temporary services use a variety of innovative recruitment, reactivation and retention techniques to attract and keep qualified people.

Temporary services have become increasingly active in training our people on such PC applications as word processing, desktop publishing, graphics spreadsheets and databases. Because these programs are constantly being upgraded and replaced, many companies have found that bringing in skilled temporary personnel is the fastest and most cost-effective way to complete projects. To accommodate client demands, we at Uniforce frequently cross train our people on a variety of the latest software packages. This makes the temporary employee more valuable to the client company, while adding to that company's productivity and profitability. Often, these temps are also used to train permanent staff.

Since the major goals of computers and office automation are greater speed, productivity and efficiency, we strive to recruit an educated and intelligent work force. At the same time, we feel that it is particularly important to maintain a humanistic perspective in this high tech age. That's why we carefully screen even the most skilled and experienced prospects for reliability, basic literacy, communication skills, past work history and appropriateness for a particular client company's corporate culture.

▌ *Why the Explosion in Temporary Employment Opportunities Will Continue*

As the need for skilled personnel grows and corporations continue to seek ways of becoming leaner and meaner, the demand for qualified temps can be expected to increase. Consider the following trends:

- According to U.S. Department of Labor statistics, over ninety percent of American businesses use temporary help. There are now almost 8 million temporary employees in an industry that has grown by an average of *18.9 percent* a year since 1970.[3]

- The use of temporary help has proven to be a highly cost-efficient measure in tight economic times. There has also been tremendous improvement in the quality and the range of services offered by temporary services.

- Temporary employees are now used by small businesses as well as Fortune 500 companies. Approximately one million temps work each week through some 10,000 temporary services. When asked what attracts them to temping, these men and women cite flexible schedules, extra income and the ability to sample work environments in various businesses.[4]

- Professions that are especially promising now for people seeking temporary employment include law, health care, computers and technical fields.

Will you be among the millions of women and men who will consider temping as a short- or long-range career option in the coming years? In the next chapter, we are going to help you start making that assessment. But right now we'd like you to meet some folks who have found that the temp's workstyle ideally suits their respective lifestyles.

Ruth, a 46-year-old mother of two college-age children, had not been gainfully employed for fifteen years. Understandably, she was anxious about reentering the workplace. Still, the family needed money to meet escalating tuition costs. Besides, Ruth felt it was time to redirect her life.

Before she had her first child, Ruth worked as a secretary. Her ability to type 90 words per minute coupled with a winning personality ensured her a choice of desirable jobs.

Now, 15 years had passed, and Ruth had lost much of her typing speed. Besides, modern offices had become automated, and Ruth felt intimidated by the very thought of a computer. If that wasn't discouraging enough, she felt out of step with the world of work.

Ruth was lamenting her predicament to a cousin, who happened to know a placement supervisor at a local temp service. Although she had reservations, Ruth called the service and was surprised to find that she was greeted warmly and invited to come for an interview the very next morning.

Although Ruth's typing skills were rusty, the placement supervisor offered her an immediate four-week clerical assignment at a local cable television company requiring light typing ability. By the end of the four weeks, Ruth had regained much of her former typing speed. During her stay, a coworker introduced Ruth to a simple word processing program, and Ruth was delighted to find that she actually enjoyed this new adventure.

Two years have passed, and Ruth is now adept at no fewer than four word processing programs. Consequently, she has her choice of high-paying temp assignments. "Temping gave me an opportunity to earn money immediately," Ruth says, with a renewed sense of confidence. "I can't believe how easy it was for me to update my skills and find success in the workplace."

Ed, a recent college graduate, was seeking a permanent position as a junior copywriter in an advertising agency. After a six-month job search, he was still unemployed and almost out of money. A friend suggested that a temp assignment as a word processor might be a good way for Ed to get his foot in the door.

Ed registered with three temp services and specifically requested that he be placed in an advertising agency. Within a week, one of the services offered Ed a six-week assignment in a top New York advertising company. Ed did a good job and made a favorable impression with the people in his department. As he developed cordial relations with his supervisors, Ed talked about his career goals.

When one of the copywriters had to take an extended leave of absence because of health problems, Ed was given an opportunity to show what he could do. He was kept on the payroll as a temp for a three-month trial period, after which he was offered a permanent job. Ed informed his service about the offer, and they were able to make appropriate and equitable arrangements with the client. During his three years with the agency, Ed has received two promotions.

Sam is a certified public accountant who took early retirement at age fifty-five. After three years of relative inactivity, he returned to the workplace as a temp and now feels more needed and respected than ever before. He is able to work at a high skill level and is energized by the idea of being a problem solver at different companies. Sam literally glows when he enumerates the benefits of temping:

"It's great to be able to generate extra income without jeopardizing my Social Security benefits. I know exactly how much I can earn, and I pace myself accordingly. My placement supervisor understands my needs and never has a problem when I refuse an assignment.

"Last year, I wanted to spend the winter traveling to several cities in Florida and California, so that I could relax in the sun. When I discussed this with my placement supervisor, she said, 'No problem.' In fact, since my temp service had offices in those cities, she was able to help me set up an itinerary that was custom tailored to my work *and* personal needs."

At age forty-seven, Phil was fired after eleven years as a financial manager at a major communications company. Unfortunately, this happened during the 1991-1992 recession, a time when thousands of people were finding themselves in a similar predicament. Nevertheless, the old bromide that misery loves company was little consolation to an unemployed man with a non-working wife, three children and a mortgage.

Aside from the financial setback, Phil also experienced a crisis in self-esteem. "It wasn't a good feeling to suddenly have no place to go after all those years on the job," he remarked. "I knew that there was virtually no chance of replacing my job in this atmosphere of massive cutbacks and downsizing. Frankly, I had no idea about what I was going to do."

Like many uninformed people, Phil never even considered temping. As far as he knew, this option was only appropriate for secretaries and clerical workers. Phil was about to find out that a growing number of executives in his field were choosing to work on a temporary basis for companies in need of their experience and knowledge.

When Phil found out that a former colleague who had been laid off at the same time was now earning a comparable salary in a temporary position, he wanted to learn more. Phil's friend actually suggested that getting fired might have

been a stroke of good luck. He talked about the new challenges of changing work environments, freedom from
cutthroat political disputes and a more flexible lifestyle that
enables him to spend more time with his family.

Shortly thereafter, Phil found a temporary position in
his field. Unlike his friend, Phil feels that he would like to
find another permanent situation. Still, he is glad to have a
place to go and a paycheck at the end of the week. He is also
making contacts that may help him in the future.

"I can't say that I'm sure just where I'm going to land,"
Phil admits. "But, while I'm finding out, temping is making it
possible for me to recover my financial viability as well as my
self-esteem. At the same time, I intend to take full advantage of
this opportunity to explore a variety of career possibilities."

Lisa is an aspiring screenwriter who hopes one day to
have one of her plays and/or films produced. She has been
chasing her dream for over a decade and has no intention of
giving up. Fortunately, she possesses technical writing skills
that have enabled her to make a comfortable living as a career
temp. Although she is based in Los Angeles, Lisa has traveled
to New York, Boston, Miami and Phoenix to pursue opportunities. In each city, she was able to temp whenever the need
arose.

"My family thinks it's foolhardy of me to keep trying to
make it in such a competitive field," she confides. "But as
long as I can support myself, I see no reason to abandon my
hopes. I must say, though, that if it weren't for temping, this
would not be possible."

Now that we've touched on some of the basics and
introduced you to a few of the 8 million men and women
who make up the growing world of temporary employment,
we invite you to continue what we hope will be an interesting
and exciting journey. Our objectives in the chapters that
follow are threefold:

1. To help you assess your particular career and lifestyle
    needs

2. To determine how these needs fit with the rapidly expanding opportunities in temporary employment

3. To work with you in mapping out a personalized temporary employment game plan

As you will see, there is a whole new world of opportunity out there. By reading this chapter, you have opened the door. We now invite you to venture further into the exciting world of temporary employment.

 ## Notes

1. *Working Woman* (June 1986).

2. 1990 U.S. Census Bureau Statistics.

3. *The Temporary Help Industry: An Annual Update,* (NATS Survey 1991).

4. At various times throughout the book, these temporary-service professionals are called *placement supervisors, staffing managers* or *personnel coordinators.*

2

*I*s *Temporary Employment Right for You?*

*I*magine picking up a newspaper and reading the following classified ad:

High Pay—Top Companies!
Qualified applicants wanted to start immediately.
Select your own hours. Paid vacations, free training
and bonuses. Call today!

Does this sounds like the kind of job you've been dreaming about? If so, you might want to consider becoming part of the rapidly growing temporary employment industry.

What's that? You say temping is an option that's never even crossed your mind? That's all about to change. Maybe you're unaware of how many interesting opportunities are out there. We'd like to take you on a tour of the businesses and institutions of America and introduce you to some of the people who work as temps. They include:

- A bookkeeper at a New York textile firm
- A bilingual secretary in Miami
- A word processor at a Dallas radio station
- A paralegal at a large Seattle law firm
- A trade show hostess in Los Angeles
- A senior programmer at an automobile manufacturing plant in Detroit
- A receptionist in an Atlanta hospital
- A technical writer at a company in Boston that manufactures video components
- A customer service representative in a Cleveland bank

If you could talk to these people, each one would offer different reasons for why they are temping:

The bookkeeper, for example, has two young children and is only available to work certain shifts. The bilingual secretary from Miami likes to spend part of the year traveling and has turned down a number of permanent job offers.

The word processor recently arrived in Dallas and wants to see what different companies have to offer, while meeting a variety of new people. The paralegal had put her career on hold to become a full-time parent. Now that her children are older, she sees temping as the best way to reenter the workplace.

Where else but in temping can you meet people who are able to fulfill so many different lifestyle and workstyle needs?

Consider our Los Angeles-based trade show hostess: She's a professional dancer who sometimes performs out of town. Then there's the senior programmer. He had taken early retirement and later decided that he wanted to work six months out of the year.

The receptionist in Atlanta had been out of the workplace for some eighteen years, during which time she had raised four children. Now that her oldest son is approaching college age, the family needs more money. Temping is making it possible for her to generate extra income.

Finally, there's the technical writer and the customer service representative—both of whom were laid off because of cutbacks at their respective companies. Neither of these men is certain about what the future holds, but both are gainfully employed as temps. Still, their lifestyle needs and economic requirements are not at all the same.

The technical writer has a wife and two children and hopes to use temping as a pathway to a permanent job. Meanwhile, the customer service representative, who is young and single, enjoys the flexibility and freedom of temping so much that he isn't at all sure he would accept a permanent position.

Do you recognize yourself in any of these profiles? Keep in mind that these people represent just a few of the 8 million women and men who work as temps in the course of a year. Is temping starting to sound like something that could be of interest to you? Before you decide, it might be helpful to explore some of the situations that seem to be most compatible with the temping workstyle.

▌ Second Income Needed

As the cost of such basics as food, housing, medical expenses and education continue to escalate, many families now find it impossible to manage on one paycheck. It appears that the family in which the father works a single job while the nonworking mother cares for the home and children is becoming a thing of the past.

According to the United States Bureau of Labor Statistics, both spouses are gainfully employed in over 50% of married-couple families—and that number is growing. Temping helps such families address their need for more money in a number of ways.

The husband who wishes to moonlight can work on temporary assignments during evening and weekend hours in order to supplement his primary income. In some families, the problem is resolved by the wife's working during the husband's off-hours while he stays home and cares for the children.

Because necessity so often proves to be the mother of invention, people come up with all sorts of creative ways to address their economic and lifestyle needs.

Mary and Sue are friends who live on the same street. Each has two young children, and both women decided that they wanted to work in order to ensure that their families would continue to maintain a comfortable living standard.

Sue and Mary had both been employed as secretaries before their children were born, though neither had any experience with computers or word processing. When a local adult-education program offered a four-week course in WordPerfect, the two friends decided that this was a good opportunity to upgrade their skills.

"I was intimidated at first," Sue recalls. "But it soon became clear that good typing skills were the most important ingredient in being a word processor. Fortunately for Mary and me, this was our strong point."

Upon completing the course, Mary and Sue called several temp services. Both were hired immediately. They were pleasantly surprised to learn that they didn't have to pay any kind of job-placement fee. At first, the two women made themselves available two days a week. Mary worked on Mondays and Wednesdays while Sue cared for both sets of kids. Then, on Tuesdays and Thursdays, the two friends switched roles. Sue went out to work, and Mary assumed the baby-sitting chores.

As time went on, Sue and Mary developed a close

working relationship with Janet, their personnel coordinator at the temp service. Both women were reliable, professional and extremely competent workers. Janet understood the arrangement the two friends had struck and did what she could to keep things running smoothly. On more than one occasion, she found another temp to fill in when family obligations prevented both Sue and Mary from working on a given day.

About three months after Mary and Sue started temping, Janet received a call from a client who was looking for a word processor who could work a thirty-five-hour week on a long-term basis. Since she had no one person who was immediately available to accept the position, Janet thought it might be a good idea for Sue and Mary to share the assignment. The two friends were receptive to this arrangement, and the client was open to giving it a try.

In case you're wondering why the client company was willing to accept two word processors in lieu of one, the answer can be stated in three simple words: *supply and demand.* It's true that many areas of the job market have been hurting in recent times. Nevertheless, there is an ongoing need for skilled temps—not only in word processing but also in a wide variety of skill areas.

In the past few years, more and more companies have come to value the contributions temporary employees can make to the success of their businesses. That's why they are willing to accommodate the need many temps have for *flex* time. As the client who consented to Sue and Mary's time-sharing arrangement so aptly put it: "We're ready to do whatever it takes to attract and keep good people."

▌ *Hoping to Have a Hit*

Creative and performing artists have long appreciated the flexibility temping allows. Most services in cities like New York, Los Angeles and Chicago work with actors between assignments, writers hoping to get their novels published, as well as singers and dancers at various points in their careers.

People in the arts need to have total flexibility so that they can be free to accept assignments in their chosen fields. The temp lifestyle works out well for these men and women. Some of our actors and singers continue to temp several days a week, even when they are performing during the evening hours.

We in the temporary employment industry recognize how difficult it can be for talented artists to make a living in these intensely competitive fields, and we're satisfied that we can play a role in helping these individuals realize their dreams. Although some people in the arts have been characterized as being temperamental, temporary service professionals have good working relationships with many performing and creative artists.

Claire is a respected New York-based pop and jazz singer. She also happens to be a college graduate who majored in accounting and business administration. Recently she stopped by the Uniforce office to pick up a check, and we asked her to talk about her experiences as a temp.

"I decided during my junior year in high school that I wanted to make music my life. It was clear even then that my love for singing wouldn't necessarily translate into enough money to pay the rent, much less enjoy a good living standard.

"I'd always been a good student, and there was never any doubt about my going to college. I figured that an understanding of accounting and business would serve me well in my chosen field, and I was right.

"Shortly after graduation, I moved from St. Louis to New York. After all, that's where the action was. Four months went by, and I still hadn't gotten my first paying job. I was living in a tiny apartment and was often reduced to eating peanut butter sandwiches for dinner.

"My savings had just about run out when I met a singer named Ann at an audition. We started talking, and she mentioned that she hadn't had a paying singing job for the past year.

'How do you make ends meet?' I asked.

'By temping,' Ann answered. 'I work anywhere from three to five days a week when I don't have a job singing. Let me tell you, it has saved my life more than once.'

"Ann gave me the number of her service, and I called the very next day. The personnel coordinator really liked my qualifications and said that she thought there would be no problem coming up with as many assignments as I could handle.

"Here I am five years later. I can say without hesitation that temping has been a godsend. I've made all sorts of progress in my singing career. I've worked on national commercials, toured Europe as a background singer with a number of superstar rock groups—even recorded my own album.

"People sometimes ask how come I still temp in light of all my credits and apparent success. The truth is that, in this field, it's almost impossible to maintain a comfortable lifestyle unless you're a superstar. Someone once compared the entertainment business to certain third-world countries. You've got very rich people and very poor people, but almost nobody who's in between.

"I've had months and even years where I made really good money as a singer. Still, I can go for long periods with virtually nothing coming in. When that happens, it's nice to know that gainful employment is only a phone call away.

"Temping makes it possible for me to maintain a positive cash flow during the slow times. I have every confidence that one day I'll make a record that winds up in the top ten. But until that happens, it's nice to know that I can temp whenever the need arises."

 ## Trying to Get a Foot in the Door

In today's tough job market, college graduates often run into what we call the experience "boomerang." They can't get a job because they lack on-the-job experience. And, by definition, it's impossible to gain this kind of experience unless you first have a job.

Temping enables young people to overcome this frustrating situation by getting a foot in the door and building their resumes. If you've ever thought that all you needed to succeed was a chance to prove yourself, temping is a great way to showcase your talents. In fact, 54 percent of all temporary employees are eventually offered permanent positions.[1]

Once you prove how skilled and productive you are, the chances of your being offered a permanent position are very good indeed. By that time, of course, you'll have catapulted yourself past the experience boomerang. Consequently, your services are likely to be in demand by other companies as well.

The best thing about this feeling-out process is that it works both ways. Just as temping gives companies a chance to try you out before making you a permanent part of the team, it also provides you with an opportunity to check them out before tying yourself to a long-term commitment.

Every corporate culture is different, just as each job opportunity has a unique set of advantages and disadvantages. Temping at several companies is a wonderful way of seeing firsthand what working there on a full-time basis is going to be like. And, while you're making up your mind, you'll continue to gain valuable experience.

Temping has proven to be especially valuable for people who want to break into tough fields such as advertising, broadcasting or public relations. But no matter what your field of interest, temping presents a rare opportunity to get the inside story on industries and companies you may be considering. Here are just a few examples:

- Temping enables law students to examine the pros and cons of working at law firms with different specialties.

- Men and women interested in hotel management can

work on hospitality assignments at top hotels and decide where they would most like to apply their talents.

- College students can temp at a number of publishing houses, advertising agencies or public relations firms before determining the place(s) they'd most like to work after graduation.
- People in highly technical areas can shop around until they find a company that best meets their professional needs. For example, computer programmers can choose companies that utilize state-of-the-art software.

Out of the House and into the Workplace

While we're on the subject of people trying to break into the job market, let's not forget the rapidly growing number of homemakers entering the workplace for the first time or after a long absence. This is yet another large group of people who've been successful using temping to brush up on rusty skills, build confidence and get a foot in the door.

There are some 14 million nonworking women caring for their families at home. This group constitutes the largest potential source to fill available jobs throughout the 1990's. In fact, it is estimated that women will fill two-thirds of all new jobs created in the 1990's. By the year 2000, working women will number a record 66 million.[2]

The temporary services industry is a leader in helping nonworking women enter and reenter the work force. We recognize that women who devote their lives to raising a family are often active in local school boards and community service activities. Many have developed tremendous organizational skills maintaining their household budgets and managing their homes.

Marilyn is a 38-year-old mother of eighteen-year-old twin boys who have just started college. Since getting married right after high school graduation, Marilyn had been a full-time homemaker. Now that her sons were away at school, she wanted to, as she put it, "see what the world of business was like."

Like many women in her position, Marilyn was concerned that her lack of experience would hold her back. When her friend Terry suggested that she try temping, Marilyn was skeptical. "I've never done anything," she told her friend. "Why should anyone hire me?"

At Terry's urging, Marilyn contacted a local temp service. The personnel coordinator with whom she spoke was reassuring. Marilyn made a good impression at her interview. The personnel coordinator could tell that even though Marilyn lacked experience in the workplace, the skills she had developed as a homemaker and mother would translate well into the world of business.

For the past few months, Marilyn has been working four days a week as a receptionist, and things are going better than she could have imagined. Her supervisors are always complimenting her on her upbeat personality and good work habits. When all the lines on the switchboard start ringing off the hook, they can count on Marilyn never to lose her composure or the smile in her voice. Every client for whom she works specifically requests that the temp service send Marilyn whenever they need a receptionist.

Marilyn is so encouraged with her newfound success that she has begun taking adult education courses in data processing and office management. "Now that I feel more comfortable in an office environment," she recently told her friend Terry, "I'm going to improve my skills so that my service can start sending me on more challenging and higher paying assignments. I've talked this over with my personnel coordinator, and she assures me that she'll do everything in her power to help me get ahead."

Do you see something of yourself in Marilyn? If so, don't let your lack of previous job experience cause you to underestimate the important life skills you possess. If, for example, you're like most homemakers, you are probably an expert at juggling lots of different responsibilities at once.

Temp services recognize how important attributes like this are in the workplace—and so do their client companies.

Make a list of the things you feel you're good at, and discuss them with your personnel coordinator. Just because you're embarking on a new venture, that's no reason to sell yourself short. Remember, temp services are looking to screen you in—not out.

Whether you're a homemaker just entering the workplace, a student trying to gain some job experience or a college graduate seeking an entry-level position, it's important to evaluate yourself the same way a temp service does: in terms of what you can do, not your limitations.

 Bored with Retirement

People today are living longer and enjoying the benefits of a healthier lifestyle. The old stereotype of a rocking-chair-bound grandma or grandpa has been replaced by a vibrant group of Americans who are bored sitting around and still feel capable of making a valuable contribution.

According to a recent survey by the American Association for Retired Persons (AARP), thirty-seven percent of its 33 million members are currently working full or part time. Furthermore, twenty-eight percent of those members who are retired say they have considered returning to work.[3] As the leading edge of the baby boom generation starts reaching retirement age, these numbers are expected to increase dramatically.

For those of you who are currently retired and thinking about returning to the work force, temping provides an ideal way for you to have a second career opportunity and to:

- Earn extra money

- Qualify for additional benefits
- Learn new skills
- Feel useful and productive
- Add structure to your life

Many retirees are finding that their pensions and social security benefits do not provide enough income to make ends meet. Even those who are financially secure often feel useless and out of the flow of life after they stop working. For these people, temping provides a substantial health benefit—one that often translates into a longer, happier life.

At the same time, it's natural for retired people to feel that they've worked hard and are now entitled to some well earned rest and relaxation. Here again, temping makes it possible to create a workstyle that is custom tailored to suit your lifestyle.

Jack, who is now 67, retired from his job as a pharmacist when he was 63. He spent the first few years of his retirement playing golf and watching TV.

"I had enough money," Jack recalls, "but after a while, I was bored out of my mind. A friend suggested that I consider temping. It turned out that there was a need for an outpatient coordinator at a local hospital who could fill in when the regular person had a day off, called in sick or took a vacation.

"Temping has really rounded out my life. I work only when I want, so there's still plenty of leisure time. I have to be careful to keep my earnings below the maximum allowed by social security. Still, the extra money is always welcome. But for me, the best part of temping is constantly meeting new people and feeling needed."

Sally had worked as a bookkeeper for the same company for 25 years. At age 59 she took early retirement. When her husband passed away four years later, Sally felt that there wasn't much in life to look forward to.

Sally's two married children and their families lived far away. Twice a year she and her late husband would go visit their children and grandchildren. But now, Sally feared that she would be an imposition.

"When my husband was alive," Sally recalls, "we would combine our family visits with trips to interesting places. But I couldn't see doing that on my own. Somehow, I needed to redirect my life."

The answer for Sally was temping. She started out working two days a week. Six months later she decided that she wanted to go visit her daughter in Florida. Sally's personnel coordinator assured her that there would be plenty of assignments waiting for her when she returned, and there were.

As it turned out, Sally's temp service also had offices in Florida. Her personnel coordinator told her that if she wanted to temp during visits to her daughter, her records could be transferred in short order and appropriate assignments would probably be available.

"I feel like I have the best of both worlds," Sally remarks. "Temping lets me do the things I really want to do—when I want to do them. Ever since I started temping, I sense that my children see me in a different light. Instead of worrying about what's going to happen to me, they're proud of the way I've revamped my life."

Sally and Jack are typical of the many retirees who are reentering the work force as temps and finding a new focus in their lives. Perhaps you or some retired person you know has been thinking about temping. If so, we'd like to allay some of the fears you (or your friend or relative) might harbor.

"People will hold my age against me."

As far as temporary services are concerned, age is not an issue. The only thing that matters is performance. When you speak to a personnel coordinator, he or she will be interested in your answering three questions:

1. What have you done?
2. What do you want to do?

3. How well can you do it?

Temp services are equal opportunity employers who welcome older men and women. You'll never have to worry about age holding you back from succeeding as a temp. On the contrary, age and experience often work in your favor. Companies have found that mature persons possess a conscientious attitude, essential life skills and a solid work ethic. That's why the vast majority of employers are eager to welcome retirees aboard.

"I'm too old to be trained or retrained."

Despite all the technological changes that have occurred in the workplace, updating your skills is not likely to present a problem. The temporary service will evaluate your skills and, in most cases, help you brush up on the latest equipment and techniques.

Furthermore, you'll never be sent on an assignment where you can't be successful. Nor will you ever be put in a position that overchallenges you in any way. You will always have the choice to select only those assignments that are right for you.

Even if you're an older person who has been out of the workplace for a long time, it's a mistake to count yourself out of the running. If you want to work and you project a positive attitude, most good temp services will find assignments for you. And once you've gotten your feet wet you'll be given opportunities to improve your skills and earn more money.

▌ *Recently Fired or Laid Off*

In the wake of massive corporate and government layoffs in recent years, the ranks of the unemployed continue to grow. The 1990's have seen top-level and middle managers lose their jobs right along with assembly-line workers and office staff. Should you find yourself suddenly out of work, signing up with a temp service may be the most practical step you can take.

Aside from providing an immediate source of income, temping gives unemployed men and women a way of making valuable business contacts, as well as an opportunity to develop skills that can make them more employable in the future. Beyond that, getting back into the work force has a number of psychological benefits.

Getting fired or laid off can be a painful emotional experience. No matter what reason you are given for being dismissed, it's natural to feel a loss of self-esteem. Temping gets you back in the game—and fast. It provides you with a place to go and the very real hope of being offered a permanent position. In fact, some of our franchised offices report that over half the people who want permanent jobs are tendered an offer within six months.

Because of the number and range of opportunities now available to temps, more and more unemployed people are opting to become career temps rather than accept another supposedly permanent position. Here's how Fran, an experienced architect, put it:

"I was devastated when I got laid off after five productive years at my former company. Now I know that there is no real job security in any corporation. It's clear that the era of the gold watch is over, so why pretend that it still exists?

"I started temping as soon as I lost my job, and I've come to appreciate the freedom this lifestyle offers. I'm making more money than some of my friends with comparable permanent jobs, and I'm free to take off whenever it suits me. Besides, I like not having to deal with the politics and games you find in so many corporations.

"It's not out of the question that I'll accept a permanent job one day. But it's going to have to be a situation that meets all my requirements. In the meantime, I can honestly say that getting fired has turned out to be one of the best things that's ever happened to me."

▌ New in Town

Phyllis is a skilled word processor who started temping for Uniforce when she lived in Los Angeles. Two years later, her husband was transferred to Kansas City. Phyllis was able to take advantage of our "Get Up and Go" program, which enables our temps to work anywhere Uniforce has an office.

When one of our temps moves to a new city, we transfer her records and work history to that city. In many cases, we are able to have an assignment waiting for that person at her new location. That's exactly what happened when Phyllis moved to Kansas City: Because she already had a good track record with us, Phyllis did not have to be reprocessed or reevaluated and was able to start working two days after she relocated.

Over the past decade, our society has become far more mobile than in previous years, and the temp industry has been at the forefront in responding to this trend. About 17 percent of the U.S. population pulls up stakes annually, making Americans the most mobile people in the world.[4]

As more women and men continue to move from place to place, temping will make it possible for them to hit the ground running by providing new job opportunities in whatever new city or town people find themselves. Nationwide services act as a touchstone—a friendly source that provides a sense of belonging for people just arriving in a new and unfamiliar location.

▌ Freedom Comes First

There are a number of reasons why America has become a more transient society. Aside from the relocation of many large and small corporations, there has been a migration from large industrial areas in the north to the sunbelt states in the south and southwest. Then, there are unfortunate circumstances like divorce or economic hardship, which sometimes force people to relocate.

There is, however, another side to this issue of mobility that is playing a major role in the growth of temping as a career option. An increasing number of men and women—especially those without family responsibilities—simply want more freedom and flexibility in their lives.

- Mark is a computer programmer who likes spending his winters in a warm climate. In the summer months he prefers being where it's cool. Temping allows Mark to move from place to place and work whenever he so desires.

- Barbara is a paralegal who wants to spend the next few years seeing the country. Her temp service works with her to ensure that she has assignments wherever she goes. Barbara also uses temping as a way of meeting interesting people in each new place.

- Janet is an experienced proofreader and copy editor who lives in New York. Once or twice a year, she likes to visit her friends who are, as she puts it, "scattered all over America."

When Janet registered with her temp service, she immediately told her personnel coordinator about her particular lifestyle preferences. Because the service was one with offices around the country, it has been able to keep Janet working wherever her travels have led.

For the most part, Janet has been placed on assignments that utilize her expertise. On several occasions, however, when Janet had an immediate need to generate cash, she agreed to taking less-skilled and lower-paying assignments until something better became available.

Now that you're better acquainted with some of the different kinds of people who temp—as well as the various work and lifestyle situations that are particularly well suited to temping—we'd like you to take a few minutes to complete a short questionnaire.

Some of you may have already decided that temping is

worth looking into. And undoubtedly, there are those of you who feel that this is not a viable option. In either case, we are confident that your needs, thoughts and feelings will come into clearer focus as you continue reading the chapters. In the meantime, it is our hope that the following questions will help you begin to answer the central question of our discussion:

Questionnaire: Is Temping Right for You?

Please respond to each question with a yes or no answer.

1. Do you consider yourself someone who is well organized?
2. Do you like meeting new people?
3. Are you a self-starter, someone who works well with minimal supervision?
4. Do you have good interpersonal skills?
5. Are you comfortable learning new routines and skills?
6. Do you like facing new challenges?
7. Are you reliable and punctual?
8. Do you get bored with routine?
9. Do you like the idea of being in control of your career?
10. Are freedom and flexibility more important to you than the security of a permanent job?
11. Do you want or need to work only certain days of the week or weeks of the year?
12. Are you fearful or having a problem entering or reentering the work force?
13. Are you between jobs?
14. Are you going to be in a city for a limited amount of time?

15. Do you need to increase your network of business and/or social contacts?
16. Do you need extra money?
17. Are your life skills more impressive than your work history?
18. Do you want to explore a number of different corporate environments before accepting a permanent position?
19. Are company-paid health and other traditional corporate benefits not among your primary job requirements?
20. Would you like an opportunity to upgrade your skills?
21. Do you need to build your resumé with more experience?

The above questions are designed to help you identify the personal traits, as well as the work and lifestyle needs that are compatible with successful temping. While there is no exact formula for success, the more *yes* answers you can honestly give, the better your prospects are likely to be.

 Notes

1. Newsday, November 22, 1992.
2. John Naisbitt and Patricia Aburdene, *Megatrends 2000,* (New York: William Morrow, 1990).
3. Retiree statistics refurnished by AARP, cited in national survey of the 45 and older population, conducted 1989 for AARP by Hamilton and Staff, Inc.
4. American Demographics (June 1990).

3

Taking Advantage of Expanding Opportunities in Today's and Tomorrow's Temporary Job Market

"Temporary help services provide skill levels ranging from laborers to doctors."[1]

If, at this point, you feel that the temp workstyle might suit your lifestyle and career requirements, the next phase of our journey will be of great interest. In this chapter, we will discuss the various opportunities that are available in temporary employment and help you assess which ones may be appropriate for you, whether now or sometime in the future.

While many other industries have been forced to cut back in recent years, there has been an unparalleled growth in the temporary employment field. In Chapter One, we briefly mentioned some of the advantages companies gain by developing a close working relationship with a temp service. We now want to take a closer look at the benefits companies reap by using temps as an integral part of their ongoing personnel needs so that you will have a better understanding of why opportunities in temporary employment will continue to expand.

There are four major reasons why virtually all American companies now use temporary help to complement permanent staffs:

1. Technological advances—particularly those related to computers and the automated office—have led to a shortage of qualified personnel. Temporary personnel services follow emerging technologies closely and are proven leaders in providing training in such growth areas.

The ability to use a personal computer (PC) and up-to-date software is becoming a necessity on most jobs. As a result, companies need employees with higher educational and skill levels than in the past. Temporary services are responding to that need by offering cross-training programs and providing personnel who are skilled in data processing.

One of our client companies on the West Coast recently converted to a new spreadsheet software package—one that was far more versatile and efficient than the program they had been using. Unfortunately, the only staff member who was adept at using this new program was forced to take an extended medical leave before she could share her knowledge with coworkers in the bookkeeping department. This left our client with a potentially costly void.

We were able to solve this company's problem by immediately supplying them with two temporaries who had extensive experience with this particular software application. Sandra and Joan were highly skilled people who were able to use the new software to complete the projects at hand, while training permanent staff members in converting to this leading-edge system.

Sandra and Joan had an opportunity to make the kind of important contribution that is fast becoming the trademark of today's temporary employee. By efficiently using these skilled temps as trainers and problem solvers, our client company reaped a significant savings in terms of both time and money.

Incidentally, both Joan and Sandra were offered permanent positions in the company's accounting department. Joan accepted the offer and has been working there for over a year. Sandra, a career temp, respectfully declined the position and continues to be one of our best problem solvers.

2. An intelligent use of temporary help enables businesses to significantly reduce recruitment, hiring and benefits costs. By working closely with a good temporary service, companies can save time, as well as dollars spent in advertising and interviewing for employees. Large services are equipped to furnish corporate clients with a data bank of prescreened, reference-checked people in virtually any requested skill category.

Temporary services usually provide liability and bonding insurance for their temps, which further protects their client companies. In addition, many services guarantee that clients will be satisfied with their temps. If, after a predetermined time period, a company is unhappy with a particular temporary employee, the service will generally replace that person at no charge.

Most major services have "smart hire" policies whereby client companies are able to "try before they buy." Should a company decide that it would like to retain the temporary as a permanent employee, it can either pay the service a cash conversion charge or keep that individual on temporary status for 90 to 180 days.

As discussed in Chapter One, temporary services are responsible for all employee benefits—including retirement, unemployment insurance and workers' compensation. In addition, many services are offering employees a variety of benefits, including vacations and medical insurance.

The National Association of Temporary Services (NATS) estimates that for every $100 spent on salary for a permanent employee, an employer spends an additional $9 for mandatory taxes and insurance, $14.40 for company-paid benefits, $12.90 for time not worked and $5.00 in hiring cost.[2] Other surveys, including one conducted by Uniforce, indicate that benefits costs can add as much as 60 percent to the base wage. Therefore, the savings a company can glean by using temporary help is considerable.

3. A judicious use of temporary help gives companies total flexibility in staffing and relief from steep fixed personnel costs. Temps have traditionally been used to fill in for permanent employees who are on vacation or sick leave. Filling these needs will continue to be an important function of most temporary services. As important as these established functions of temporary services are, however, they present only a partial picture of the ways services help their clients address their ongoing staffing needs.

By using temps during busy periods and for specific projects, companies are able to operate with lean permanent staffs during normal work load periods. More and more companies are now using temporaries when they start new projects, add new departments or upgrade their computer hardware or software. We in the temporary services industry are committed to helping our corporate clients meet their fluctuating needs by providing as few or as many temps as circumstances may warrant.

The Digital Equipment Corporation (DEC) is an example of a company that has learned to make judicious use of temporary employees. DEC maintains about 20 temporaries on a more-or-less permanent basis as "floaters" who work in whatever department they are needed. Some 60 temps are frequently rehired for use in specialized areas, such as the legal department. In addition, the company brings in 800 to 900 temporaries daily to fill a variety of needs.

The primary reason DEC employs so many temps is that it "doesn't want the hassles and expense of finding, hiring, and managing such a large group."[3]

4. Companies that work closely with a temporary service to address their staffing needs continue to find new and innovative ways to use temps, including:

- Utilizing the skills of back valuable employees lost through mandatory retirement
- Using the services of independent consultants (in IRS parlance, 1099 wage earners)
- Filling vital jobs during hiring freezes
- Smoothing the transition of business relocations
- *Outsourcing*—using temps to staff entire departments that are outside of their mainstream business

As we approach the twenty-first century, we expect that the temporary help industry will continue to expand as companies meet the challenges of a shrinking labor market, escalating costs and the overall demand for increased productivity in a global marketplace. Temporary help will be an important element in companies' planned-staffing strategies as they seek to cope with fluctuating business cycles and try to get more cost-effective productivity from their operations.

Now that you've seen the many advantages businesses derive by using temporary employees, the next question many of you are probably asking is: What does all this have to do with me?

For one thing, if there wasn't an explosion in the demand for temporary employees in a wide range of fields, many of you would not be reading this book. And, frankly, there is a good chance that we would never have been motivated to write it.

The fact is that the demand for temporary employees is on the rise in almost every job category. This surge reflects the evolving needs of business and industry for greater flexibility in addressing economic and market challenges, shifting workloads and vacancies. The temporary help industry doubled between 1982 and 1992, and we fully expect this growth trend to continue into the twenty-first century.

To sum up, then, the prospects are bright for those of you who may want to seek temporary employment now or in the future. And, as we discussed in Chapter Two, there are any number of personal, professional and financial reasons why many of you will, at some point, select the temp workstyle option, which brings us to the next logical question:

Is there a demand for people with my talents and abilities?

Although we have never met most of you in person, we feel comfortable making the following statement: If you have a positive attitude and really want to work, there will almost definitely be a place for you in the growing world of temporary employment.

Whether or not the assignment utilizes your highest skill level or offers the kind of remuneration you are after are issues we explore in Chapter Six. In any case, we take great pleasure in confidently assuring you that work is available.

To help you assess relevant temping opportunities, we now explore the various fields and professions that employ temporary personnel and evaluate these job opportunities in terms of current and future demand, necessary skills, experience, earnings potential and lifestyle options.

 Finding Your Niche in an Ever-Expanding Marketplace

Opportunities in temporary employment are generally divided into the following categories:

1. Automated office
2. General office/clerical
3. Marketing/sales
4. Legal support
5. Accounting support
6. Health care
7. Technical
8. Industrial
9. Professional
10. Consultants (1099 wage earners)

■ *Office Jobs*

Office jobs have long been the mainstay of the temporary help industry. There are more available temping jobs in this category than any other, and this is not likely to change in the foreseeable future.

The following sample of twenty-four occupational titles in the office sphere is by no means complete. Listed from highest to lowest average wage, it demonstrates a sampling from a range of hundreds of skills that are in constant demand:

1. CAD/CAM
2. Designer
3. Paralegal
4. Systems analyst
5. Data base manager
6. Desktop publisher
7. Spreadsheet specialist
8. PC operator
9. Full-charge bookkeeper
10. Assistant bookkeeper

11. Administrative assistant
12. Legal secretary
13. Executive secretary
14. Bilingual secretary
15. Secretary with steno
16. Proofreader
17. Transcription typist
18. General typist
19. Data-entry operator
20. Receptionist
21. Switchboard operator
22. Mailroom clerk
23. Bar-coding clerk

Without question, the greatest demand for office temps is in fields requiring data processing and computerized office skills. In fact, it is safe to say that the automation of the corporate office is the single most important reason for the unparalleled growth of the temporary help industry. Here's why: During the 1970's and 1980's, businesses came to recognize that computerized equipment would greatly speed up many of their operations. Consequently, they invested heavily in hardware and software. What many companies quickly discovered, however, was that they lacked the skilled personnel to run this high-tech stuff.

The dilemma that one family-owned electronics company was faced with in 1981 was typical. Frank, the company's CEO, had attended an office equipment show in Chicago and was "blown away" by the efficiency of computers and word processing software. He proceeded to replace his electric typewriters with computers that employed what was then considered state-of-the-art word processing software.

"Most of my secretaries were crackerjack typists," Frank recalls. "There was no doubt in my mind that they would pick up word processing in a matter of hours. After all, the people demonstrating it at the show in Chicago made it look easy. Besides, I was told that this particular word processing package was 'user friendly.'

"It didn't take me long to find out that the only things that are truly user friendly are toasters and TVs. But in the world of the automated office there's virtually nothing that you can simply plug in and use. Computer hardware and software all require some degree of training, particularly when you're dealing with people who've never operated that kind of equipment before." By automating his systems before his staff was ready to use the new technology, this well intentioned CEO had created a productivity gap that threatened to erode his company's profits. We helped Frank bridge this gap by furnishing temporary personnel who could both operate the software and train the secretarial staff to use it.

As anyone who is the least bit familiar with computers knows, there is always a new and improved piece of software or hardware that will get the job done even faster and more efficiently than the one that is presently being used.

Like many astute executives, Frank continues to upgrade his company's office equipment whenever such changes appear to be warranted. But now he consults with us in advance so that we can provide him with the skilled temporaries he needs to maximize productivity and minimize transition costs.

Rapid changes in office technology continue to fuel an increasing demand for skilled temporaries. Since the corporate world has come to rely on temporary services to furnish people with these skills, it is in our interests to respond accordingly.

In previous decades, temps were used primarily for lower-end clerical and secretarial functions. As a result, they were considered to be relatively interchangeable and disposable. This has all changed—thanks, in great part, to the automated office.

Today, when a temporary service finds a highly skilled person who is also dependable and has good communication skills, it does its best to hold onto him or her. At Uniforce, we've learned that the same principle holds true for a growing number of our client companies.

With the rapid advancement of technology, it is becoming exceedingly difficult for even the biggest and best temporary services to maintain an inventory of skilled people who are facile on all the required hardware and software packages. In order to keep up with a diverse and continually changing client demand, a growing number of temporary services have opted to invest in employee training and cross-training programs.

If you have skills on one popular PC software package, many good temporary services will cross train you on other programs. At Uniforce, we offer cross-training through self-taught tutorials on computers in our offices.

Typically, we make appointments with the people we cross train and allow them to come in and use our equipment. When an individual feels confident, we evaluate her on the newly acquired skills to assess whether she is ready to be sent out to client companies. We are currently offering cross-training on more than fifty packages, including:

- DOS
- Windows™
- Microsoft Word™
- WordPerfect™
- Lotus 1-2-3™
- dBase™
- Paradox™
- DisplayWrite™
- MultiMate™
- WordStar™
- PageMaker™
- Excel™
- Framework™

The specific software packages will depend on the service and its assessment of current client demand. Before you are eligible for any sort of training, you may be required to work a specified number of hours for a temporary service. This policy varies from service to service, as do the degree and type of training and cross-training offered.

Many of the better services believe it is wise to invest in upgrading the skills of their people. There are, however, some services that take the position that they are not in the business of training and do not wish to devote time and resources in this direction. More about this in Chapter Six.

In general, the outlook for temporaries with office skills is quite good. Those of you who are just getting started in office temping may find it useful to seek assignments in a number of companies that have different kinds of automated equipment. If you already possess typing skills, you may be able to learn a popular word processing package in a few short weeks by taking an appropriate adult education course at a local high school or community college.

Depending on your area of interest, office skills can be applied in virtually any field. The following is just a partial listing of industries and businesses that use large numbers of temporaries with automated-office skills:

- Law firms
- Advertising agencies
- Insurance and real estate companies
- Banks and financial institutions
- Publishing houses
- Health care organizations
- Airlines
- Retail firms
- Educational institutions
- Utilities
- Telecommunications companies

If these or other fields hold particular interest for you, be sure to inform your placement supervisor. Keep in mind that exposing yourself to a variety of office environments will give you a more well-rounded look at the different uses of office automation.

The more adept you become at using in-demand software packages, the more well paying options you will have. Skilled career temps who have no interest in working at one place for very long generally have their choice of plum assignments. Those of you who are thinking about long-term or permanent assignments will also find that opportunities abound.

Once you demonstrate your job skills and your ability to fit into a particular corporate culture, you'll find that companies will be very hesitant to phase you out. They've learned how difficult it is to recruit and replace good people. That is why companies continue to request skilled temps back on a consistent basis.

A few years ago, the typical assignment for a highly skilled person averaged about two weeks. Now, it is common for such assignments to last three months or more. The overall elevation in status of temporary employees has benefited all concerned—the employee, the temporary service and the corporate client.

We're well aware that many of you may not possess the kind of up-to-date technical skills demanded by the automated office. If that's the case, we'd like to urge you not to be discouraged. Everyone is looking for people with common sense, basic intelligence and good communication skills. In fact, these abilities are usually all that are necessary to get you started working for a temporary service, even if you have no PC experience or don't know how to type.

It is not uncommon for companies to hire people with no keyboard or typing skills for data entry positions. The only requirement is the ability to input information accurately. If you do have typing skills, many temporary services will train you on a PC after they've employed you for a period of time.

The bottom line is: There are temporary jobs for almost everyone. It is projected that, in the next few years, literate, entry-level people with even minimal skills will become scarce. As a result, beginning temporaries can expect to be in a better bargaining position than in the past. If you are reliable, have good people skills and are willing to work at least two to three full days a week, that's all it takes to get rolling.

If you like the office environment, there are almost always receptionist and basic clerical positions available. In fact, we believe that one of the largest growth areas for opportunities in the future will be for clericals with good communication skills. Are you someone who fits this description? And are you willing to put some effort into learning automated-office skills? If so, this can be a great way to get your foot in the door.

▌ Marketing Jobs

These are often a good choice for men and women who tend to shy away from computers and office equipment but who like interacting with people. As a rule, marketing positions are also handled by services that concentrate on office assignments. There are also a number of services that maintain separate marketing divisions. This wide-ranging category of temporary work includes such job titles as:

- Telemarketer
- Salesperson
- Product demonstrator
- Convention host/hostess
- Trade show support person
- Pollster

Jack is an aspiring actor who has minimal office skills. For the past six years, he has supported himself through a variety of temporary marketing assignments. Jack recently shared some of his experiences with us:

"I've been working on a long-term telemarketing assignment for a company that purchases remnants from mills in the Southeast and sells them to manufacturers around the country. I've also worked as a Santa Claus during the past five Christmas seasons, and I really enjoy that. I consider myself an extrovert who loves interacting with people.

"Recently, I was trained to operate a robot that entertains at parties and gives out product samples at trade shows. I stand about ten feet away and operate the robot electronically. In a way, it's sort of like being a ventriloquist. I can make the robot move its legs, arms and head. There's even a way to make it seem like the robot is talking or singing. Aside from some basic acting and vocal abilities, I'm responsible for working the electronics and making any needed repairs on the spot.

"In this kind of temporary work, the pay varies as much as the assignments. When I operate the robot, I sometimes earn as much as $20 an hour. On the other hand, I average about eight dollars per hour on my current telemarketing job. Still, because I temp through a number of services and am always willing to try something new, I can work as much as I want.

"Last year, I had an out-of-town acting job in Chicago. When it ended, I registered with a temp service, and immediately landed a job conducting a marketing survey for a local television station. After the play closed, I stayed in Chicago for the next two months and supported myself temping. This kind of workstyle is great if you like adventure and meeting new people."

▮ *Industrial Jobs*

Industrial jobs tend to be cyclical and seasonal. Such jobs have a high turnover and generally require little skill or experience. And while the pay scale for this kind of work is relatively low, such "jeans" jobs are often a practical choice for students and others who lack office skills.

The greatest demand for industrial temps comes from manufacturing companies. Much of the work in this area requires simple assembly-line functions. Because of the repetitive nature of such jobs, employee burnout is an ongoing problem. People tend to become bored and inefficient at their tasks and frequently have to be replaced.

Much of the work in the industrial temping field is short term. While there is likely to be an ongoing need for industrial temps, we do not consider this a particularly desirable alternative for highly educated people or those interested in temping as a career. However, these jobs do offer students and others who may lack office skills the opportunity to earn extra money. The following is a partial listing of job titles in the industrial area:

- Assembly-line work
  - Bagging
  - Sorting
  - Inserting
  - Packaging
  - Quality control inspection
  - Ticketing
  - Food service person
  - Material handler
  - Shipping/receiving clerk
- General laborer
- Maintenance custodian
- Janitor

- Mailroom assistants
- Inventory clerk
- Loader
- Security guard

▌ *Health Care Jobs*

Health care jobs are on the rise, and this trend is expected to continue well into the twenty-first century. In fact, medical and technical fields are projected to be the two most rapidly expanding segments of the temporary services industry. As a result of advances in medicine and greater public awareness of the benefits of nutrition and physical fitness, people are living longer. Consequently, they require more varied and frequent medical attention.

Before the early 1980's, most health care temps were assigned to hospitals. More recently, governmental and private medical insurance providers began limiting coverage to a specified number of days for each treatment or procedure. As a result, hospital patient stays have been greatly reduced.

In the future, it is expected that the majority of temporary employees in the health care field will report to nursing facilities, convalescent centers and patients' homes. Of course, there will always be hospitals, and they will continue to use temporaries for the same reasons as other modern corporations.

By keeping a small permanent staff supplemented by as many temps as are needed to meet a patient population that fluctuates on almost a daily basis, hospitals are able to significantly reduce their fixed personnel costs while effectively addressing their immediate needs.

Nursing and home health care are projected to be the two largest growth areas in this occupational category. Before 1980, nursing was considered a secure profession that attracted many women. During the early years of that decade, however, hospitals began reducing their nursing staffs. At the same time, opportunities in other career areas started opening up for women. Consequently, by 1990, there was a 40 percent shortage of qualified registered nurses.[4]

Dr. Ona Robinson, a New York-based psychologist who specializes in women's career issues, sees the nursing shortage as an outgrowth of the women's movement:

"In the past," she notes, "women who sought careers were encouraged to enter one of two: nursing and teaching. These were occupations that utilized traditionally feminine caretaking skills and posed no direct competitive challenge to men.

"Thanks in part to the efforts of feminists, talented and ambitious women have now achieved success in virtually every professional field. And while there are still some inequities in dollar compensation and glass ceilings that make it hard for women to reach the very top in certain fields, there are enough successful role models to prove that virtually anything is possible."

There are, of course, still women—and, for that matter, men—who consider nursing their career of choice. These individuals are essentially in the driver's seat in terms of selecting from a large number of temporary and permanent job opportunities in virtually all geographic areas.

The home health care field has been growing by approximately 15 percent annually in the 1990's. In 1993, the industry is expected to gross over $18 billion.[5] The growth of the home health care field will continue to accelerate as a result of three socioeconomic trends:

1. People are living longer and are, therefore, more likely to experience periodic illnesses. As a result, they may be fully or partially incapacitated for days, weeks or months at a time.

2. The cost of inpatient hospital care has become prohibitive, even for those families with extensive medical coverage. As a result, more and more treatment and recovery take place in the home setting.

3. In an increasing number of American families, aging

parents are no longer able to live with their grown children. Even in those families where such a live-in situation is feasible, both spouses are likely to have jobs. Consequently, outside help is often required.

Depending on the kind of home health care that is needed, there may be partial or full reimbursement from Medicare/Medicaid or a private health insurance provider. If, for example, the attending hospital physician deems it essential that a nurse visit a discharged patient's home several times a week, full or partial compensation may be due.

In a growing number of cases, however, the cost of temporary home health care will not be covered by governmental or private medical insurance. A person recovering from surgery, for example, may not need a nurse. However, he or she may require an aide to administer medication, prepare meals and provide assistance getting in and out of bed. More often than not, families have to pay for these temporary services out of pocket.

In addition to assisting patients recovering from surgery, health care aides and companions may provide short- or long-term assistance to a handicapped person or to an individual who is frail and elderly or terminally ill.

People who perform such home health care functions are generally referred to as companions or home health care aides. Remuneration for these health care services varies widely, depending on geographical area, a person's experience and certification. In general, the pay is comparable to what one would earn for industrial or entry-level office work.

Unlike other clients of temporary services, families who hire temps to provide medical assistance usually do so on a one-time basis. Many states have no specific requirements for people wishing to be companions or health care aides. Nevertheless, people who do this kind of work often take short certification courses from the temporary service or a local hospital. Depending on the nature of the patient's needs, an assignment can last anywhere from a week to a year or more.

The following is a partial list of temporary job titles in the health care field:

- Registered nurse
- Licensed practical nurse
- Nurses aide
- Dietitian
- X-ray technician
- Laboratory technician
- Orderly
- Attendant
- Home health care aide
- Companion

 ## Technical Temporary Jobs

Technical jobs include such occupations as engineers, chemists, computer analysts and quality-assurance inspectors. Demand for these positions has been positively impacted by the computerization of the corporate world. Electronics firms, automobile manufacturers, aerospace firms and ship builders are among the high-volume users of technical temporaries.

In the wake of the dissolution of the Communist bloc in eastern Europe, there has been a significant decrease in defense work. We expect this to have a somewhat adverse impact on the demand for technical temporaries. Nevertheless, manufacturers must continue to take advantage of new technologies if they intend to remain competitive. Consequently, the outlook for people seeking temporary employment in technical occupations is quite favorable.

Most temporary jobs in the technical field are contingent on specific contracts assigned to a corporation. Therefore, deploying temporaries on a per-project basis makes good business sense. Technical temporaries are rarely hired to replace permanent employees who are sick or on vacation. Rather, these carefully screened professionals are retained as integral parts of skilled teams who work on difficult, often sensitive projects. In general, experienced people are coveted, both by the client and the temporary service. They are hard to find and even more difficult to replace.

It should come as no great surprise that technical temporaries can earn significantly more money than their counterparts who do similar work on a permanent basis. In general, though, the corporate client does not provide health insurance, vacation or retirement benefits, although some of these perks may be furnished by the temporary service. (More about this in Chapter Six.)

The following is a partial listing of occupational titles of temporaries in the technical field:

- Architect
- Computer programmer
- Computer analyst
- Network engineer
- Chemical engineer
- Civil engineer
- Electronics engineer
- Industrial engineer
- Systems analyst
- Drafter/designer
- Laboratory technician
- Technical illustrator
- Technical writer

■ *Professional Temporaries*

These can now be found in virtually every field. A growing number of attorneys, doctors, pharmacists, accountants and corporate executives are all taking advantage of the freedom and flexibility that temping offers. Take a look through the yellow pages of the telephone directory for any major city, and you'll find listings for services that specialize in each of these fields. Keep in mind that it is often not necessary to live in the city where that service is located, since many of these services have clients in all areas of the country.

In fields like medicine, law and accounting, you're not likely to find many professionals who refer to themselves as temporaries. More often than not they will call themselves consultants or independent contractors—which brings up an issue that has become a major concern to both our corporate clients and employees.

In recent years, the IRS has become increasingly vigilant in monitoring companies who do not list independent contractors (or 1099 wage earners) directly on their payrolls. Some companies and consultants have been hit with multi-million-dollar fines for violating the applicable statutes. The intent of these punitive measures is to discourage companies from using the Independent Contractor classification. As a recent article in *Forbes* notes, the IRS's reasoning is simple to discern:

"(Consultants and other independent contractors) are required to pay the full Social Security/Medicare tax on their earnings, up to the maximum of $10,658 a year. But when such a worker is classified as an 'employee,' he or she owes half the tax and the employer owes the other half.

"Whoever pays, the amount of revenue to Uncle Sam is about the same. But the IRS doesn't (look favorably upon) independent contractors and fights to reclassify them as employees on the firm's books. Why? Because independents are far (more likely) to underreport income. . . . Figuring it's easier to audit firms' payrolls and 1099 filings than to look through millions of individual's bank accounts, the IRS tries to get as many (people as possible reclassified) as employees."[6]

Many companies are finding that the best way to avoid such complications—while still retaining the valuable services of consultants and other professionals—is to set up a customized, comprehensive program with a temporary service or other third-party employer.

Under such an arrangement, independents are regarded as employees of the temporary or other payrolling service, which, in turn, assumes the employer's tax responsibility. To help clients assess their specific needs and avoid tax problems, Uniforce has established an affiliate called *Payroll Options Unlimited, Inc.*

While the number of professional temps still accounts for a relatively small percentage of all temporary employees, the rapid growth of this segment of the industry has served to elevate the prestige of the entire field. It is now clear that temping is a workstyle that can be geared to virtually any career and lifestyle.

What, you may be wondering, would induce a doctor, attorney or other status-conscious professional to work on a temporary basis? As with temps in other areas, there are as many reasons as individuals you ask. But, for the most part, the motivation for giving up the stability that comes with permanence is the flexibility and freedom that come from being able to work when and where you want to work.

Law is one of those professions where success can require putting in a 70-hour week. David is a typical attorney who graduated law school, landed a job as an associate with a large firm and "worked his brains out" to become a partner. Once David achieved this goal, he found that he was working even longer hours than before.

"One day," he recalls, "my wife broke the news that she was suing for divorce. Among her most bitter complaints was that I was a workaholic who paid no attention to her. I remember looking in the mirror and realizing that I was 58 years old. "Why did I spend the past 35 years killing myself? I wondered. I always told myself that I was doing it for my wife and kids. My success allowed me to give my family everything—at least from a material point of view. Obviously, I'd been neglecting some other aspects that in retrospect may have been more important."

David's story is one that is repeated countless times a day—over lunch or in the offices of psychotherapists and physicians. But today more and more people are learning from the mistakes of David and people like him: They are selecting quality of life over bigger bucks.

Like David, 40-year-old Max was a partner in a top New York law firm. Max was considered one of the most talented and dedicated attorneys in his field, and his hefty salary reflected this status. After 15 years of putting in 60–70 hour weeks, Max began suffering from intermittent chest pains and chronic sleeplessness. Max's doctor did not find any physical cause for these symptoms. However, she did suggest that such problems are often related to a stressful lifestyle.

While Max was relieved to learn that he wasn't seriously ill, he wasn't quite sure what to do about his doctor's advice that he restructure his lifestyle. One evening, as he was having dinner with Marilyn, an attorney who maintained her own small practice, the following conversation took place:

"I can never make the kind of money you do," Marilyn admitted. "But I enjoy working for myself. Lately, things have been slow, so I've been supplementing my income by working on a temporary basis doing research and trial preparation work for a firm that specializes in litigation.

"I find this kind of law interesting. But, frankly, I'd never consider getting involved with the kind of pressure and politics it takes to survive at a large firm."

"I envy you," said Max, shaking his head in exasperation. "I wish I could just leave my firm and start my own practice. It must be great to work at your own pace and be able to combine your personal and professional life to suit your needs. I wish I could do that."

"You sound as if you don't have any choices," Marilyn said. "But you could do something like what I'm doing if you really wanted to."

"No way!" Max responded. "I would probably starve. I don't see how I could possibly go out on my own."

Marilyn told Max bluntly that, while starvation was highly unlikely, he would have to take some risks and make some sacrifices if he was going to revamp his professional life and hold onto his health. She assured him that, in the end, the rewards would be well worth the short-term anxiety such an upheaval was likely to create.

As you might imagine, it wasn't easy for Max to relinquish his partnership in the high-powered firm to open up his own small practice. But when he thought of everything that was at stake, he realized that there was no choice.

Slowly but surely Max is building his business to the level at which he will be comfortable. Whenever he runs into a slow period, Max is always able to find temporary work through the same service that places Marilyn.

Max fully realizes that he will never earn the kind of money he was making before, but the trade-off is more than worth it. Between his own clients and the temporary service, Max averages a 25-hour week. Now that the pressures and stressful politics are removed from his life, Max feels great, both physically and emotionally.

When a friend recently asked Max what he does with all that time he used to spend working, his answer was simple, "Whatever I want!"

Don is a 50-year-old physician who worked in large urban hospitals for most of his career. About three years ago, he felt he was burning out and knew he needed to make a change.

"Another physician originally told me about working on a temporary basis," Don recalls. "He's a semiprofessional jazz musician and likes having time to pursue this love.

"Unlike my friend, I don't have any particular passion in another field. Still, my children are grown, and I'd been divorced for ten years. Since I had a certain amount of freedom, I figured that this was a good time to take advantage of it.

"I decided that I would enjoy traveling to different parts of the country. At the same time, I didn't want to retire. I may feel differently in a few years. But right now this workstyle is ideal. Last year, I worked approximately eight months. This year, it's going to be more like six months. Next year, who knows?"

Kathryn is a registered nurse with two school-age children. "I don't want to be tied down to a permanent job—at least not while the kids are still young," she says. "Temping allows me to fill in at a number of hospitals near my home. I have a good relationship with my service, which allows me to work as much or as little as I want."

Cutbacks and downsizing left thousands of mid-level and senior executives unemployed during the early 1990's. As a result, financial executives are among those professionals who have recently been entering the field of temporary employment in growing numbers—though not necessarily on a totally voluntary basis.

Jeffrey is a former financial manager who had been working for the same large corporation for 20 years. At age 61 he was induced to accept a fairly generous early retirement package.

"Basically I had no other choice," Jeffrey recalls. "My company provided me the means to live comfortably, although not at the same level I was able to afford at my salary. In any case, money wasn't the main issue. I felt that I still had something to contribute and would never have considered retirement.

"When a former colleague of mine referred me to a temporary service that had placed him on some interesting assignments, I must admit that I was skeptical. But after speaking to the people at the service, I realized that it was time to rethink my options.

"A few weeks later, the service offered me a temporary position with a company that was far smaller than the one where I had been employed. I was hesitant at first, but now I'm just thankful that I didn't let this opportunity slip by.

"I'm working on my third long-term temporary assignment, and making a very respectable salary. And while there are no pension and less comprehensive health benefits, the work is far more exciting than anything I'd been involved with in my old job.

"At these smaller companies, my know-how and experience are truly valued. I love the challenges of changing work environments periodically and the freedom from the kind of political disputes and backbiting I had to confront nearly every day at my old job. I've also decided to take several weeks' vacation between assignments, and this has given me the flexibility to spend more time with my family and friends. At this point, I don't think I'd accept a permanent position, no matter what the salary."

■ Notes

1. *Modern Office Technology,* February 1991.
2. *Ibid.*
3. *Fortune.* February 15, 1988.
4. U.S. Department of Health and Human Services statistics.
5. Cited statistics are derived from a study by The Omnicomp Group in the NATS Survey, *Contemporary Times,* Winter 1990.
6. *Forbes,* March 2, 1992.

4

Working with a Temporary-Employment Service

One essential key to successful temping is establishing and maintaining a good working relationship with one or more services. Remember, your temporary service is, in effect, your employer, so you always want the people there to think well of you. Still, in many respects, the association between you and your service goes well beyond the traditional boss-employee relationship.

We are not aware of many work situations that allow you to design a work schedule around your specific needs and preferences. The temp workstyle is unique in that it is custom-made for people who want to call their own shots.

Do you only want to work six months out of the year?

No problem. Do you enjoy having summers off? That's fine, too. Would you like to earn a living while checking out the lifestyle in a variety of locales? If so, the temp workstyle is made to order for you. By the way, if you want to work a five-day week on a year-round basis, you'll probably be able to do that as well. The choice is yours.

Another unique aspect of the temp workstyle is the ability to have an open-ended relationship with one or more services. Imagine telling your boss in a conventional job situation that you'll work for him as long as you're comfortable. Then, if the mood strikes you, you'll take a couple of months off, and then go to work for another company. Most employers would fire you the moment they overcame their disbelief.

If, on the other hand, you stated the same conditions to a placement supervisor at a temporary service, she would most likely say: "That's fine. Just let me know in advance what your plans are."

If you'd like, you can work for one service for a period of time, then switch to another if, at some point, they are better able to meet your needs. You can accept a long-term assignment for a period of time, go on an extended vacation, and, at any point, let your service know that you want to start working again.

As long as you act reliably and inform your service of when you will and will not be available, the temp workstyle will enable you to build in as much freedom and flexibility as you require.

As with any business relationship, there are some basic guidelines that will ensure smooth and successful dealings between you and your service. The best way to think of your association with a service is as a partnership based on mutual need. The service needs you to do a good job at client companies so that it will be called upon in the future. By the same token, you need a temporary service to give you the best assignments when you want them—and to help you build your resumé and experience.

There are various kinds of services from which you can choose. Out of the approximately 10,000 temporary service offices nationwide, some—like Uniforce—are owner-operated franchise locations or branches of large national companies. There are also a number of large, independently owned firms that maintain multiple offices, as well as smaller companies that operate out of single locations. One of our goals in this chapter is to show you how to select the service(s) that can best fill your needs.

 ## *What Kind of Temporary Service Is Right for You?*

As a temporary employee, you have the opportunity of working with many kinds of services. There are services that specialize in such areas as automated office skills, data processing, accounting, technical, scientific, legal and medical assignments. There are also many general services that can offer assignments in a broad range of clerical and light industrial skills. Some temporary companies advertise "temp-to-perm." If you know in advance that you are looking for a permanent position, be sure to ask about that aspect of a service.

One question we are often asked when we speak to people who want to start temping is: "Am I better off working with a general or specialty service?" Whichever service you choose, there is usually very little downside risk. Still, an informed choice can save you time and effort.

There are advantages to both kinds of services, depending on your particular needs and objectives. You can elect to sign up with both a general and specialty service if you wish. If, however, you want to work in a specific job area, you may be better off with a service that specializes in that field.

With a specialty service, you are more likely to be placed on assignments that utilize your highest level of skills. You may even have your choice of companies, which will enable you to receive valuable exposure and on-the-job experience. Specialty services are often able to offer higher pay rates since their corporate clients usually request people with more specialized and higher-level skills.

If, on the other hand, you are more flexible about the kinds of temporary assignments you are willing to take, a general service might be a more suitable alternative. This is particularly true if you want to be sure that you will always be working. Let's look at two workstyle situations that called for different solutions in terms of selecting a temporary service.

Ethan is a recent college graduate who is about to enter a Ph.D. program. All through college he worked through a temporary service that maintained a large inventory of general assignments.

"I've worked as a data-entry clerk, a telemarketer, a clerk-typist and a sorter at a manufacturing company," says Ethan. "The jobs are never the same, but my service can always keep me working whenever I need extra money.

"After graduation, I told my assignment supervisor that I wanted to earn as much money as possible before I left for graduate school. She found me a full-time summer data-entry job at a local hospital. This is one of the better-paying temporary jobs I've had. But even if this weren't available, it's good to know that my service would have found me some kind of money-making assignment."

Martha is a second-year law student who wants to sample conditions at a number of law firms before deciding on where she wants to apply. To help her accomplish this, she has been working as a paralegal through a temporary service that specializes only in the legal area.

"I have no interest in any other kind of temp work because I feel that it won't further my overall career goals," Martha says. "But by temping as a paralegal I've been able to get a firsthand look at a variety of law firms from the inside while making valuable contacts. Temping has helped me earn extra money working only when I want to work. And, because my service specializes in my area, I'm never called for an assignment in another field."

Martha's assessment of the advantages of a specialty service are pretty much on target. While many general services would be able to provide her with assignments in her chosen field, it is likely that they would not be able to come through with as many assignments in a particular area of expertise like law. Consequently, someone like Martha would not have the opportunity to gain the experience she needs to achieve her long-term objectives.

Again, we want to stress that it is hard to envision much of a downside whether you choose a general or specialty service. If the general service tells you that they can keep you busy with assignments in your field, you'll find out soon enough if that assessment is correct. Should that turn out not to be the case, you can move to a service that is able to meet your requirements.

A Word about the Disadvantages of Temping

Several years ago, there was a popular TV commercial that put forth the slogan: "Try it, you'll like it!" Perhaps it would be too glib to apply this same witticism to temping. Nevertheless, we honestly believe that for a great many of you temporary employment can provide the workstyle solution to your lifestyle needs. As with anything in life, however, there are some disadvantages to temping, and it would be remiss of us not to mention them.

If you are concerned with career pathing or upward mobility within an organization, temporary employment is not likely to be your best alternative.

By definition, working as a temp means that you won't gain the tenure needed to become eligible for profit-sharing programs, retirement plans, medical and other company benefits. If, of course, your temporary job leads to a permanent position in that company, you're talking about a whole new ball game. But this is an objective you can set going in.

Some temps complain that they are not treated as well as permanent employees performing similar functions. Fortunately, these complaints are becoming less common as temps continue to prove their value and gain in status.

For some people, another downside of temping is produced by the constant change in their work environments. There is bound to be a certain amount of stress involved whenever you start a new job. Some people experience such changes as challenging. Others feel anxious about having to develop rapport with new coworkers, as well as a sense of loss that comes from having to give up positive relationships that took time to develop. Men and women who enjoy temping seem to relish working at different companies and meeting new people.

There are, of course, some built-in limitations to the kinds of relationships you are likely to attract when you work on a temporary basis. If, for example, you're looking for a mentor, temping is probably not your best alternative. Such relationships are difficult to nurture since an experienced person is less inclined to mentor someone who could be leaving at any time.

While all of these complaints have a basis in reality, it is important to recognize that everything in life involves some kind of trade-off, whether you're dealing with a marriage, a business decision or a job. But interestingly enough, we are meeting more and more people who actually see much of the downside of temping as an upside.

There are more women and men who are choosing temping as a career (for a complete discussion of career temps, please see Chapter Seven). For these individuals, nothing can match the freedom and flexibility that are unique features of the temp workstyle.

Most major services have special programs for career temps that include medical and vacation benefits (for a complete discussion of benefits available to temporary employees, please see Chapter Six). Can these match the extensive benefits packages offered by large corporations to their permanent employees? Perhaps not, but most career temps don't feel the need to have a high level of company-provided medical coverage or a comprehensive corporate retirement plan. Furthermore, they enjoy meeting new people and facing new challenges—advantages that come from temping at different companies.

 ## A Five-Step Plan for Selecting a Temporary Service

Although your initial commitment to a service is not particularly substantial, it is important to make your choice with care. Many of you will be coming into contact with the temporary services industry for the first time, and it's important that you have a positive experience. To help you become a good consumer when you shop for a temporary service, we are going to take you through the process step by step:

STEP ONE: OBTAIN THE NAMES OF SEVERAL SERVICES IN YOUR AREA

If you had to find a physician or attorney, you would first try to get referrals from friends and relatives you trust. This way, you'd have the advantage of speaking to people who've had firsthand experience in dealing with a particular individual or firm.

The same principle applies when you are looking for a temporary service. Do you know anyone who has had experience temping? If so, ask them what service or services they work for. Ask them to describe how they've been treated at each service. Tell them what your objectives and expectations are. Then ask if they would recommend a particular service, and why.

If you are a student or a recent graduate, you might consider asking someone in your job placement or career guidance department for referrals. Perhaps they know of one or more reputable temporary services that have done a good job finding assignments for qualified people.

Please don't worry if you are unable to generate the names of temporary services through personal or professional referrals. Virtually every service can be found in your local yellow pages, generally under such headings as: "Employment Agencies" or "Employment Contractors—Temporary."

Many services also advertise in the classified section of local newspapers and trade publications. Some services also conduct open houses, during which prospects can discuss their resumés with placement supervisors and management representatives in an informal setting. Attending such functions affords you the opportunity to ask questions, meet other temps and gauge the environment at various services.

STEP TWO: SCREEN EACH SERVICE OVER THE PHONE

Once you've compiled a list of three or more services, the best course of action is to call each one to set up an appointment. You may notice that some newspaper ads state that no appointment is necessary. Nevertheless, we think it's a good idea to take this extra step. After you've started working with a service, much of your contact will be over the phone, and your first phone conversation can tell you a great deal about what those interactions will be like.

Here are some things to take note of during that initial phone call:

- How is the phone answered at the various services you call?

- Is the person on the other end polite and considerate of your time?

- Does she mention the name of the service?

- Does she mention her own name?

- Are you kept on hold for a long time?

- Do you feel like you're being treated as a valued customer?

All of these seemingly small cues can speak volumes about a service's professionalism and the overall attitude it has toward the people who work for the service. A professionally run temporary service recognizes the potential value you have to its business. At Uniforce, the management and staff are fully aware that the temps who work for us are more than just employees. When all is said and done, they are our valued customers—as much as our corporate clients. After all, if we are unable to supply good people to fill a client's needs, it will soon be taking its business to another temporary service.

Since the main purpose of the initial phone call is to help you develop a general impression of how a service operates, it's usually a good idea to save most of your specific questions for your in-person visit. You may, however, want to ask the following questions in the course of the phone conversation:

- In what kind of assignments does the service specialize?
- Does the service have immediate assignments in your field?
- Can you obtain specific directions on how to get to the service's offices?

It's important to keep in mind that, during your initial phone call to a service, they will be screening you just as you are screening them. Therefore, you should make it a point to be polite, articulate your questions well and respect the time of the person on the other end of the line.

STEP THREE: DO SOME INVESTIGATING

Once you've made your initial phone calls, you might want to take the time to make an unofficial visit to each service on your list—at least those that made a favorable impression over the phone. Dropping into the offices unannounced will give you a chance to take a first-hand look at the operation. In many cities, different services maintain offices in the same geographic area. Such proximity gives you an opportunity to visit several in the course of a day.

The best times to make these anonymous visits are on a Monday morning—when a high volume of assignments is usually handed out—or on payday. During these busy times you can usually remain incognito as you continue to size up the operation of your prospective employer. Here are some questions these brief sojourns can help you answer:

- How do the temps (your potential coworkers) at this service impress you?

- Do they look and act professionally?

- How are they being treated by the temporary service staff?

- How large is the staff working at the service?

- In general, does the operation seem to be well organized and professionally run?

While you're on the premises, be sure to pick up the service's brochures and other promotional literature. Read these materials over carefully. A service's promotional literature will generally reflect, among other things, the number of years it has been in business and whether or not it has a national affiliation.

We feel that a service with a national affiliation is generally able to offer more, particularly if there is a chance that you will be temping in a number of different cities. But, as in all businesses, some temporary services are better than others.

Whatever its size, you want to be associated with a service that has a good reputation as an employer in the community. Most of the better temporary services belong to the local chamber of commerce and are an integral part of the communities in which they are based. Often, they will be involved with community activities, participate in charitable fund-raising and sponsor sporting events and/or teams. You may want to call your local Better Business Bureau and ask if there have been any complaints against a particular temporary service. There's a saying: Good news travels fast, but bad news travels even faster. Ask around, and you will most likely find someone in your circle of relatives, friends and acquaintances who has worked for that service. You can learn a great deal by asking them such basic questions as:

- How were you treated?
- What kind of assignments did you receive?
- Were you able to work when you wanted?
- Were you well compensated for your work?

It would probably be impossible to find a single company in the world that could claim 100 percent satisfaction among all its employees and clients. Nevertheless, most of the better temporary services have good reputations and will usually be given high marks by present and former employees—as well as by other sources in the community.

One way to ensure that the service with which you are affiliated is reputable is to ask whether they belong to the National Association of Temporary Services (NATS). Founded in 1966, NATS provides legal, legislative, regulatory and industry-related activities and information on behalf of its temporary service members. NATS is supported by more than 1,100 temporary help companies operating over 8,100 offices nationwide.

We strongly recommend that you work with a service that is affiliated with NATS. Member services are bound by a code of ethics with respect to their treatment of employees. NATS also produces a wide range of written materials about the temporary help industry. You can contact NATS by writing or calling:

National Association of Temporary Services
119 South St. Aseph
Alexandria, VA 22314
(703) 549-6287

STEP FOUR: SET UP APPOINTMENTS FOR IN-PERSON INTERVIEWS

At this point, you should be ready to make appointments for interviews at the services on your list. While there are a number of similarities between a temporary service interview and one with a conventional employer, there are some key differences. First let's talk about some of the similarities:

Appearance counts: A clean, well-groomed, professional appearance is critical when you are applying for a job at a temporary service—as it is for any job interview. By professional, we're talking about donning attire that is appropriate for the kind of position in which you would like to be placed. If, for example, you are applying for an executive secretarial position, it would be wise to go for the temporary interview in a business suit, especially if you'd like to be placed in a large company.

If, on the other hand, you are a student applying for a summer position, you have the right to request an assignment at a company that does not require you to wear conventional business attire, or you can ask to be placed in an assignment that is back office, or in a "jeans job" where you don't have to dress up.

In such situations, clean and casual attire will do for the interview. No matter what kind of job you are seeking, however, we strongly suggest that you don't show up dressed in jeans. If you are flexible about the kinds of assignments you're willing to accept, dress for the one that will require the most businesslike attire.

Common sense dictates that people show up well groomed and appropriately dressed for the job they are seeking. Nevertheless, we are sometimes amazed at how often this basic rule of thumb is ignored. Don't make the mistake of allowing a bad first impression to narrow your opportunities.

The major temp services sometimes have visual or written orientation materials to apprise new employees on the importance of dressing appropriately and adhering to the dress code of the companies to which they are being sent. At Uniforce, we also cover these points in our *Welcome to Uniforce* brochure, which is given to our new temps and covered verbally during discussion with their personnel supervisors.

Attitude is critical: As much as possible, try to relax. Take an open, friendly approach to the proceedings, but stick to business. Answer all questions in a concise manner. Listen carefully to make sure you answer the questions exactly as they are directed at you.

Temporary service coordinators are usually pressed for time and need to ascertain the vital information necessary to place you on the correct assignment in as short a time as possible. That's why it's essential to listen carefully and answer each question accurately. Make it clear from the start that you respect your interviewer's time, and she will reciprocate the favor.

Honesty is always the best policy: There can certainly be no disagreement with this statement from an ethical standpoint. Nevertheless, people often feel they have to exaggerate their qualifications or previous experience when looking for a job. We realize that it's tough out there, but we believe that people who take liberties with the truth do themselves and their employers a great disservice.

Ethics aside, there is absolutely no reason to be less than completely honest when interviewing with a temp service. As we've stated before, the temporary service needs you. Consequently, they are looking to screen you in—not out.

It's important to remember that when you're interviewing for a temp service you are not being considered for any one job. You can be sure that the placement supervisor is going to try hard to find you an assignment where you will be happy and motivated to perform at your best. That's why there's no need to be anything less than honest about your previous experience.

Keep in mind, however, that there is a big difference between being honest and revealing extraneous or inappropriate information.

When answering questions, be concise. Give only the nature of the responsibilities you had with previous employers and your accomplishments. Please don't discuss the internal politics of your former companies, the faults of your previous supervisors or the nature of a company's strategies. This is good advice for any job interview and particularly one with a temporary service.

It's important to keep in mind that the interviewer is only interested in *you*, so keep the interview self-directed. As much as possible, leave out the word *we* and stick to the word *I*. For example, a good response to the question: "What did you do on your last job?" would be:

"I was an executive secretary for Mr. Howsman who was the President of the ABC company. In that capacity, I took dictation, transcribed and made his personal appointments. I left that position because my family moved to another state."

Conversely, an inappropriate response to that same question would be:

"At the ABC Company, we were actively involved in developing new products. My duties were administrative and secretarial, but this was only small part of what we were trying to achieve as a department. Eventually, my boss was forced to take early retirement as part of a corporate coup. After that, things were never the same, so I quit."

The above response contains too many extraneous details. It wastes the interviewer's time and may cause her to question your judgment and professionalism. Temporary service interviewers use what we call *"can do, will do* fit" criteria for applicant selection. This means that they are primarily interested in answering three questions:

1. Can you do the job?
2. Are you motivated to do the job?
3. What kind of corporate environment will you fit into?

Whatever the interviewer's assessment of your *"can do, will do* fit," she may ask you to accept an alternate position until she can provide you with the kind of assignment that you really want. But, again, you can rest assured that the service will do what it can to place you on an assignment that you like and for which you are qualified.

STEP FIVE: MAKE THE MOST OF YOUR TEMPORARY SERVICE INTERVIEW

If you've done well on interviews for permanent jobs in the past, you should have no problems interviewing for a temporary service. Still, there are some unique aspects of a temporary service interview that we'd like you to keep in mind.

There are two key differences between a temporary service interview and one for a permanent position:

1. The temporary-service interview probably will not take as long.
2. You'll probably walk away with a job.

When you interview for a permanent job, there is usually one job opening and a closed-end result: You either land the job or you don't. On the other hand, when you interview for a temporary service, you walk in knowing that you are not going to be confronted with a do-or-die situation.

Most major temporary services have assignments available at all skill levels. Even if you don't land the primary position for which you apply, it is likely that you will be offered some kind of assignment. This aspect of temping is particularly helpful when you want or need to start working immediately.

It's important to recognize that, even after you've established yourself with a service, there may still be times when the assignment supervisor is unable to provide you with a position at your highest skill and salary level. When that happens, you can do one of three things:

1. Turn down the assignment and wait until something better comes along.

2. Call another temporary service and see if it can fulfill your needs.

3. Accept a less-desirable position with the understanding that it's only temporary.

These options are just part of the reason why temporary employees cite flexibility as one of the most appealing aspects of this workstyle.[1] Flexibility is also a key to the mutually beneficial relationship that can exist between you and your temporary service. And remember: It all starts at that initial interview.

There is no question that, in a sense, you and the temporary service are auditioning each other. Nevertheless, the interview process should be relatively short and stress free. Most reputable services strive to make the initial interview as pleasant as possible by creating an environment that makes prospective employees feel comfortable and secure. Light refreshments are often available, and you can even expect to be offered a small gift, such as a pen or sun visor.

In addition to making you feel comfortable, a good temporary service wants to impart as much basic information as possible during your visit. To accomplish this, it will give you one or more pamphlets that answer often-asked questions about payment, training programs, bonuses and benefits. The written materials may also address what the service expects of you in terms of dress, attendance and deportment at client companies. You may also be asked to view an employee-orientation video.

Most temp services will ask you on an initial interview to refer friends, relatives or acquaintances who may be looking for a job. In exchange for these referrals, they offer bonuses when that person's assignment is completed. Here again, you are being presented with still another opportunity to benefit yourself and the temporary service.

During the course of a temporary-service interview, you can feel free to ask questions and make demands that would be unsuitable when interviewing for a permanent position.

Imagine telling a potential employer who was considering you for a permanent job: "I want to work Monday, Wednesday and Friday days at large service-based companies." Your assignment supervisor may or may not be able to immediately accommodate this specific request, but you can be sure that she will do her best.

▌ *Questionnaire: Sizing up a Temporary Service*

Aside from the suggested list of questions that follow, we encourage you to pay careful attention to a service's professionalism. As noted earlier, this attribute can be quickly gauged by taking note of the appearance of the office, the appearance and attitude of the people in the office and the general efficiency of the operation.

During the course of your stay at the service, take note of the amount of personal attention you receive. Did your interviewer block out a specific time for you, or were you expected to sit and wait until you were called?

Take a close look at the content and quality of the literature and other welcome materials you are given. Has the company been in business for a long time? Do these materials make you feel good about the service and the people who work there? Don't underestimate the importance of your first impressions. They often turn out to be correct.

When you leave the premises of the temporary service, it is important to walk away with a sense that this is the beginning, not the end, of the story. Did the interviewer give you his business card and invite you to call any time if you should have questions? Did he tell you when your next contact is going to take place?

The following is a list of suggested questions you may want to ask at an interview with a temporary service. It is quite possible that you won't find it necessary to ask every question, or you may think of additional questions that are not included here. In general, though, these are the questions that are most commonly on people's minds:

1. Are you a general or specialty service?
2. Do you have a choice of assignments for which I qualify?
3. How soon can you send me out on an assignment?
4. Can you keep me working regularly?
5. Can you give me assignments that utilize my highest skill level?
6. What is the pay range for the kind of work I do?
7. How and when will I be paid?
8. What kinds of training and cross-training programs do you offer?
9. What kinds of bonuses and benefits do you offer?
10. What kinds of companies will you be sending me to?
11. Will I have a choice of work environments?
12. Will I have a choice as to how I'd like to dress?
13. Do you have special programs for career temps?
14. Do you have a temp-to-perm program?

15. If I travel or move, do you have affiliated offices in various cities to which you can forward my records?

 ## What a Temporary Service Wants to Know about You

The objective of a temporary service interview is to obtain a picture of you as a total person. The service is as concerned with your attitude, appearance and ability to communicate as with your specific skill levels. Your interviewer is a trained professional, skilled at pinpointing a prospect's qualifications in a relatively short period of time.

When you arrive for your appointment, you will be given a number of forms to fill out. For your reference, we have included this on pages 90 and 91.

You will first be asked to fill out a *preemployment application* in order to determine the type of work-history card you will be asked to complete.

The work-history card also serves as an employment application, which will help the interviewer assess why you are seeking temporary work, your skills, and the kind of commitment that you might be giving to a particular temporary position.

Be sure to fill out your work-history card completely. State what your previous temp and permanent work experience were. Put a check next to all of the equipment and software you can operate. Extra space is usually provided so that you can add any additional skills or equipment that may not be listed.

The interviewer is looking for complete information. This includes all of the things that you can do and the length of time that you have done them. Whenever possible, be sure to specify exact dates, so that your interviewer can ascertain how current your experience is.

Your interviewer will stick fairly close to the materials on the work-history card when talking to you. These are the questions you can expect to be asked—either verbally and/or in writing:

- Why are you seeking temporary employment?
- How did you hear about this service?
- Have you ever worked for this service?
- Do you require an accommodation to perform the job function for which you have applied?
- Do you have access to transportation necessary to get to assignments?
- What days and hours are you available to work?
- Can you start an assignment immediately?
- Can you accept assignments on short notice?
- Other than minor traffic offenses, have you ever been convicted of a crime?
- Are you willing to submit to preemployment testing for drug and alcohol use?
- Are you interested in long-term assignments?
- Are you interested in a permanent position?
- What is your work history?
- What is your educational background?
- What are your skills?
  What type of assignments would you prefer?
- Are you prepared to take skill-assessment evaluations today?

While the service is asking for a good deal of information, there is no reason to feel intimidated or overwhelmed. Most of the better services strive to make the entire interview process a pleasant and illuminating experience.

Remember, the temporary service is trying to determine the type of assignment for which you would be best suited, based on your needs and skills. The reasons for some of the above questions are self-explanatory. Others may seem confusing or unnecessary. Therefore, let's take a moment to review why certain information is important to a service and, ultimately, to you.

A service wants to know why you are seeking temporary work in order to assess the kind of commitment that you might be willing and able to make to a temporary position. If, for example, you are a student looking for a summer job or someone who is going to be moving to another city in a month, the assignment supervisor will not be seeking anything that might have a long time frame.

The interviewer wants to know how you heard about the service in order to ascertain the effectiveness of its various advertising efforts and referral sources. The better services put a good deal of time and effort into this aspect of their business, so your feedback is greatly appreciated.

It's essential to let your interviewer know if you have ever worked for the service—whether at this or another location. If so, you may not have to complete the paperwork because the records can usually be transferred in short order. Most national services have a work/travel program to accommodate the growing number of people who, for one reason or another, move around from place to place. At Uniforce, we call this our *Get Up & Go* Program.

A temporary service needs to know if you have the ability to get to and from work and whether you have any geographical preferences. It is important to a service that its employees get to work on time, and your access to transportation is one indication of how long you will need to travel to assignments.

By asking the days and hours you are available to work, the interviewer will be able to assess whether you can handle full-week assignments or just full days. She will also be interested in knowing whether or not you would be available for second or third shifts and weekend assignments, which are often available through temporary employment services.

Keep in mind that you must work a minimum of two full days a week. Also, there is usually no part-time work at temporary services, although 5–9 P.M. telemarketing and data-entry positions are sometimes available.

Since temporary services frequently have open job orders waiting for people to come in, they consider it a plus if you can start an assignment immediately. Likewise, your willingness to accept an assignment on short notice will also enhance your desirability. Temp services receive many client requests on short notice. That's why they value temps who are easy to reach and willing to be sent out immediately.

In the long run, availability can be the key to your success as a temporary employee. Sometimes choice assignments come in at the last minute, and it is opportunistic for you to let your service know that you are available on short notice. Temporary services understand that on occasion this may interfere with other things you have going in your life. On the other hand, your availability may be the catalyst that puts you in the right place at the right time when that dream assignment comes across your placement supervisor's desk.

Whatever your availability, it is desirable to have a telephone-answering machine attached to your phone, preferably one that lets you pick up messages when you are out. At this writing, an answering machine equipped in this way can be purchased for as little as $50.

It is important for a temporary service to know if you have ever been convicted of a crime. The purpose of this is not to judge or condemn you, but to ascertain whether the nature of the offense will prevent you from being bonded for a particular position. If you do not wish to be sent out on any assignments that require preemployment testing for use of illegal drugs and alcohol, please say so.[2]

We've mentioned before that, in most cases, a temporary service is less concerned with where you've been than with what you are able to do. Nevertheless, you can expect to be asked in-depth questions about your previous work history—with respect to both temporary and permanent positions. This information gives the personnel coordinator a profile of your stability and reliability, as well as sources for references.

If you have been employed and have a work history, you will want to bring a resumé or list of jobs you have held with the names, addresses, telephone numbers of previous supervisors and the last salary you made before you left. By providing complete information, you will ensure that the interview process will go far more smoothly. If you've worked for other temp services, make sure to include the dates and the client companies to which you were sent.

Most temporary services will be ready to accommodate you if you are a student with no previous work history. If that's the case, you can bring personal references from teachers, clergy and coaches. You should also bring a list of any student affiliations, clubs, volunteer work or extracurricular activities in which you may have participated.

Take a little extra time when filling out the section of the work history card that asks you to check off those skills in which you have work experience. This is a particularly important section in helping your interviewer determine the kinds of assignments and payment for which you qualify.

In addition to assessing your requisite skills, the interviewer is interested in the kind of work you would like to do. This information will help her determine the various skills evaluations you will be taking—as well as the kinds of companies that might have openings for you. If you indicate that you are prepared to take skills assessment evaluations that day, the interviewer will factor that into her time schedule.

When you fill in the part of the work-history card that deals with education, be sure to include not only your primary education and high school but also any business, vocational or trade school that you have attended. Don't forget to specify whether you received a degree or certificate from any of those schools. Include any college or advanced degree education you may have had. And, again, don't forget to mention whether you received a degree.

In order to complete the work-history card, you will need to sign it in two places: One signature confirms that you have read the company drug-free workplace policy; the other verifies that the information you have given is accurate and complete. Remember, this form must be filled out completely for your personnel coordinator to proceed to the next step of the interview process—the skills assessment evaluations.

■ *Five Test-Taking Tips*

1. Remember, You and Your Service Have Mutual Interests. In approaching a temporary service's skills assessment evaluations, it's important to keep in mind that their objective is to screen you in—not out.

The sole purpose of these instruments is to evaluate your exact skill levels. By carefully analyzing the results, the experts at the service will be able to place you on assignments that you will enjoy, while satisfying their clients' need for temporary employees whose performance meets or exceeds expectations.

2. Take a Positive Approach. Even though you may feel nervous, try to relax and give it your best shot. You are not in school anymore, and you're not going to be graded. Remember, there is no report card here—only a job at the end of the tunnel. Besides, you can always take these tests again at another time.

Lapses of memory are normal in test-taking. If you feel blocked when attempting to answer certain questions, go on and come back to them later if time permits. In any case, don't expect to answer every question correctly. In fact, some of the evaluations are constructed so that the average applicant will not answer all of the questions correctly.

3. Use Your Time Wisely. Look over your evaluation before you start working, and try to get a feel for its length and difficulty. Plan your time. If, for example, you have a time limit of 10 minutes for a 20-question evaluation, check that you are beyond question 10 after the first 5 minutes.

Work as quickly and carefully as possible, but don't be a clock watcher. Clock watching will use up your time and make you more anxious. Very often, you will be in a testing area that is not isolated. Try to focus on the questions—not on what's going on around you. Some services want to see how you handle the distractions you are likely to encounter in work environments that are less than serene.

Remember, on most tests, easy questions count just as much as the more difficult ones. If you have time, you can go back to the questions you left out the first time.

4. Pay Close Attention to All Directions.   If you are not clear about any portion of the instructions, ask so that you know exactly what is expected of you. Be sure to complete the sample questions that appear at the beginning of the test, even if you feel certain that you understand what is required.

Read each question carefully, no matter how simple it appears to be. Make certain that you know exactly what you are being asked to do. On multiple-choice questions, read each choice before you answer. There may be instances where the correct answer is not absolutely correct but is the best among the choices you are given. Be sure to consider and compare all the choices before picking the one you believe is best.

5. Avoid Careless Mistakes in Marking the Answer Sheet.   If the answer form does not line up directly with the test, you might be putting your answer in the wrong row for your question. If you change an answer, make sure you have thoroughly erased your first response. Most often these evaluations are done in pencil, so making changes is not difficult.

Let us reemphasize that the service wants to place you in the best and highest-paying position possible. If you are not satisfied with the results of your evaluation, ask for an opportunity to practice and brush up on your skills. Then, come back and try again.

◼ How Many Temporary Services Do You Need?

As we mentioned earlier, there is no reason to limit yourself to one temporary service, at least when you first start out. We encourage you to apply to a number of services and see which one can best address your needs. Is a specialized or general service for you? Why not register with both and see what happens?

As you progress in your career as a temporary, you are likely to find that you are most comfortable working with one particular service. But, again, one of the things that enhances that comfort is the knowledge that you can go elsewhere should you feel the need or even the inclination to switch. In any case, the decision is yours.

The following evaluation form is designed to help you assess the various temporary services you visit. We suggest that you complete the form each time you interview with a service and update the information as the need arises.

◼ Temporary Service Assessment Profile

Name of service:

Address:

Telephone number:

Date of first phone call:

How contact was established:
   (Yellow pages, classified ad, personal/professional referral)

Person(s) spoken to:

General/specialty service:

Date(s) of informal visit(s):

Impressions:

Interview appointment date:

Name of interviewer:

Skills evaluations administered:

Assignment(s) offered:

Pay range:

Benefits:

Bonuses:

Training/cross-training programs:

Overall impression of service:

Whichever temporary service or services you decide to work with, the principle of mutuality holds. It's in a service's best interest to treat you fairly and with respect. If it does otherwise, you'll soon start earning money for another temp service. At the same time, a lack of reliability, a bad attitude or poor work habits will not put you in good stead with your service—or with your supervisors and coworkers on the job.

Always come to appointments and assignments well groomed and on time. Look people directly in the eye, speak audibly and project yourself in a positive light. For the most part, temporary employment services want to help you achieve your workstyle and lifestyle objectives. It is in their best interests to say *yes*. Don't put them in a position where they are forced to say *no!*

▌ *Notes*

1. NATS Survey, *Contemporary Times,* Winter 1990.

2. More and more companies are requiring that services pre-screen applicants for evidence of drug or alcohol use. In those instances, temps may be required to sign an authorization and release-from-liability form. This

form is intended to prevent temps who are not willing to consent to be drug tested from being assigned to clients who require such testing as a condition of employment.

"*Get Ahead in Style*"

Come to the *free* "GET AHEAD IN STYLE" seminar and learn the simple but vitally important image techniques that can help you gain instant recognition and respect.

Are you hurting your chances to succeed by projecting the wrong image?

Did you know that the first three seconds count more than the following thirty minutes in making a good first impression?

SEMINAR FOR SUCCESS

This *free* seminar will demystify the look of success and show you the appropriate clothing, accessories, hairstyles and more that will help you, or someone special in your life, "Get Ahead In Style." You'll also find it doesn't cost a fortune to look like you're worth one!

UNIFORCE *SERVICES*

DATE: _____ PLACE: _____

TIME: _____ R.S.V.P. BY: _____ CALL: _____

UNIFORCE® SERVICES

WORK HISTORY CARD

SKILLS | 1 | 2

| Name (last) | First | MI | Home Phone | Message/Business Phone | Today's Date |

| Street Address | City | State | Zip Code |

Form W-4 Department of the Treasury Internal Revenue Service
Employee's Withholding Allowance Certificate
▶ For Privacy Act and Paperwork Reduction Act Notice, see instructions.
OMB No. 1545-0010
1993

Why Are You Seeking Temporary Employment?

How did you hear about Uniforce?

| 1 Type or print your full name | 2 Your social security number |

Home address (number and street or rural route)

City or town, state, and ZIP code

3 Marital Status
□ Single □ Married
□ Married, but withhold at higher Single rate
Note: If married, but legally separated, or spouse is a nonresident alien, check the Single box

Have You Ever Worked | When? | Where?
For Uniforce?
YES □   NO □
Type of assignment you would prefer.

Do you wish to be considered for assignments that require pre-employment testing for use of illegal drugs and alcohol?
YES □   NO □

4 Total number of allowances you are claiming (from line G above or from the Worksheets on back if they apply) .
5 Additional amount, if any, you want deducted from each pay .
6 I claim exemption from withholding and I certify that I meet ALL of the following conditions for exemption:
• Last year I had a right to a refund of ALL Federal income tax withheld because I had NO tax liability; AND
• This year I expect a refund of ALL Federal income tax withheld because I expect to have NO tax liability; AND
• This year if my income exceeds $500 and includes nonwage income, another person cannot claim me as a dependent.
If you meet all of the above conditions, enter the year effective and "EXEMPT" here ▶ 6 19
7 Are you a full-time student? (Note: Full-time students are not automatically exempt.) . 7 □ Yes □ No

Other than minor traffic offenses, have you ever been convicted of a crime?
Yes □ No □ If yes, explain. (Each case is individually considered.)

Do you require an accommodation to perform the skills identified below?   Yes □ No □

Under penalties of perjury, I certify that I am entitled to the number of withholding allowances claimed on this certificate or, if claiming exemption from withholding, that I am entitled to claim the exempt status.

Employee's signature▶   Date ▶   19

Person to Notify in Case of Emergency

| Phone | Address | City |

Are You A Student?
YES □   NO □
Are you able to get to and from a job site?
Yes □   No □
UNIFORCE is an Equal Opportunity Employer M/F/H/V

TO BE FILLED IN BY PERSONNEL COORDINATOR UPON ACCEPTANCE OF FIRST ASSIGNMENT

THIS BOX FOR OFFICE USE ONLY

I-9 completed □ 3 yr. anniv. date _____ ID exp. date _____

Month and Day of Birth /
Mo.   Day

● UNIFORCE SERVICES, INC.
F-805-487 (Rev. 12/92)

CHECK ONLY THE SKILLS IN WHICH YOU HAVE WORK EXPERIENCE

TYPING:
□ Electronic (memory) □ Electric
Make & Model   How Long?

□ Correspondence □ Proposals
□ Manuscripts   □ Statistical
□ Policy/Claim   □ Invoice
□ Purchase Orders Typing from:
□ Checks   □ Handwritten
□ Tax Returns   (copy)
                  □ Typed (copy)
□ Other
SPECIAL TERMINOLOGY:
□ Legal □ Medical □ Engineering
□ Finance□ Other
□ Bilingual–Language:
___ speak   ___ write
___ translate ___ read
□ Other

SECRETARIAL:
□ General   □ Executive
□ Administrative □ Steno
□ Fast Long Hand □ Speedwrite
□ Machine
Transcription
equipment:

OFFICE SKILLS AND EQUIPMENT:
□ Proofreading □ Reception
□ Filing–___ alpha ___ numeric
□ Copier   □ Teletype
□ Facsimile   □ OCR
□ Mailroom   □ Postage Meter
□ Addressing   □ Collating
□ Coding   □ Inventory
□ Microfilm/Microfiche
equipment:
skills:
□ Other

TELECOMMUNICATIONS:
□ Telephone System (ex.: Centrex
Horizon, Dimension)
Equip Name-# of Lines—How Long?

___ relief ___ full time
□ Telex/TWX □ Other ___
AUTOMATED OFFICE
Complete OA Supplement for:
□ Word Processing □ Data Entry
□ Spreadsheet   □ DOS
□ Data Base Management
□ MIS Complete MIS Supplement
SALES AND MARKETING:
□ Booth Attendant □ Merch. Display
□ Host/Hostess   □ Product Demo
□ Survey Taker   □ Phone Sales
□ Telemarketing   □ Direct Sales
□ Initiating   □ Shopper
(Outbound calls) □ Model
□ Receiving   □ Cashier
(Inbound calls)
□ Other

ACCOUNTING: How Long?
Complete Accounting Add-On
□ Bookkeeper
___ Asst ___ F/C □ Gen. Ledger
□ AR □AP   □ Trial Bal.
□ Dbl Entry   □ Sgl Entry
□ Bank Recs   □ Posting
□ Payroll   □ Cred. & Coll.
system:
No. People ___
□ Manual   □ Computer
□ 10-Key Calc./Add Mach.
___ touch ___ sight
□ Bank Teller □ Accountant
Acct. Equip. Used—How Long?

MISCELLANEOUS:
□ MIS–Complete MIS Supplement
□ Draftsperson □ Engineer
□ Librarian   □ Messenger
□ Quality Control
□ Lab Tech–type:
□ Catering–skills:
□ Other

□ I will accept same day assignments.   □ I am available for long term assignment.   □ I am interested in a permanent position.

Dates Available for Work
start _____ until _____
Circle Days Available
M T W T F S S
Day Hours From _____ to _____
Night Hours From _____ to _____
SOCIAL SECURITY (verified □)
□□□-□□-□□□□

DO NOT WRITE BELOW THIS LINE. PLEASE CONTINUE ON THE OTHER SIDE.

CLERICAL	LANG. SKILLS							
Alpha	Spelling	F/C BKKP.				COMMENTS AND RECOMMENDATIONS		
Numeric	Punctuation	ASST. BKKP.				Min. Hrly. Rate $		
Proofreading	Grammar	Appearance	E	AA	A	BA		
Classifying	Vocabulary	Attitude						
GEN. TYPING	BUS. TRANS.	Communication						
ROUGH DRAFT	LEGAL TRANS.	Speech						
STAT. TYPING	MED. TRANS.	Job Knowledge						
STENO	ALPHA/NUM. D.E.	Exp. Level						
10 KEY	NUMERIC D.E.	Geog. Preference:				Interviewed by:		

PLEASE ANSWER ALL QUESTIONS

EDUCATION (Circle Highest Grade Completed)	High School	1	2	3	4	General Equivalency Diploma ☐			

Business/Vocational School _____ College 1 2 3 4 4+

Skill or Trade _____ Degree or Major _____

PREVIOUS PERMANENT EMPLOYMENT

DATES		Name/Address of Company	Phone Number	Supervisor	Type of Work	Salary	Reason for Leaving
From	To						

PREVIOUS TEMPORARY EMPLOYMENT

DATES		Temp Service Name/Town	Companies Where Assigned	Supervisor and Dept.	Skills	Pay Rate
From	To					

I have been given a copy of the Uniforce Temporary Services Substance Abuse and Drug Free Workplace Policy to read. I understand that I may ask any questions I wish regarding its contents and that if I am employed by Uniforce I agree to abide by this policy.

WITNESS   APPLICANT'S SIGNATURE   DATE

I hereby affirm that all information given by me on this Work History Card is true and complete. If my answers are untrue or misleading, you have the right to dismiss me immediately. If selected for employment, I agree to provide documentation showing that I am authorized to work in the U.S. You may contact my former employers for references and release the information received and contained on this Work History Card to your clients and insurance companies and may give references on me. If I work for you, I will be your employee. I will obtain permission before discussing permanent employment with your clients. I will keep confidential all information I learn from your clients. I will notify you when my temporary assignments end. If I don't, it means that I am not available for work. I understand that my employment may be terminated at any time for any reason and that you will only be liable to me for wages earned up to termination.

DATE _____ APPLICANT'S SIGNATURE _____

PLEASE DO NOT WRITE BELOW THIS LINE

REFERENCES CHECKED	Company Name	Phone ☐ Mail ☐	Company Name	Phone ☐ Mail ☐	Company Name	Phone ☐ Mail ☐

CLIENT NAME	REPORT TO	JOB DESCRIPTION	PAY RATE	BILL RATE	START DATE	EST. DUR.	FINAL DATE	EVALUATIONS				CONTACT LOG DATE/COMMENTS
								E	A A H	A	BA DISMISSED/REASON	

BIRTH MONTH	NAME (Last, First)	PHONE / TOWN	WPM	STAT	SEC	TRANS EQUIP	S H	SPEC TERM	TEL COM	CLK	PRF	D E	W P C	P	ACCT	MIS	TECH	MKTG	LT IND

≡●≡ UNIFORCE°
≡U≡ SERVICES

LANGUAGE SKILLS EVALUATION

NAME:_____

DATE:_____

PART A - SPELLING

Place a check next to the words that are spelled incorrectly.

Examples:	Acident	_____		Genuine	_____

1.	Accomodate	_____	11.	Posess	_____
2.	Appearence	_____	12.	Privelege	_____
3.	Beginning	_____	13.	Receipt	_____
4.	Benefitted	_____	14.	Seperate	_____
5.	Description	_____	15.	Successful	_____
6.	Experiance	_____	16.	Toogether	_____
7.	Independent	_____	17.	Truely	_____
8.	Necesary	_____	18.	Until	_____
9.	Occurrance	_____	19.	Who'se	_____
10.	Opportunity	_____	20.	Yield	_____

PART B - PUNCTUATION

Place a check next to the sentences that are punctuated incorrectly.

Examples: Correct punctuation is essential. _____

Effective writing, and speaking are important. _____

1. The contractor completed all work on time. _____
2. When can our company expect your proposal: _____
3. Please process the following order, lumber, tools, nails, paint. _____
4. The individual was hired on Friday, March 22, 1959. _____
5. The manager delivered her speech and immediately left for the airport. _____
6. The departments meeting will take place after lunch today. _____
7. Although the vice president was to decide today he deferred his decision until next week. _____
8. Mrs. Smith we wish to express our apologies. _____
9. Please send us thirty-five, 35, sets of materials. _____
10. Our delivery driver will pick up the package at 9 00 A.M. _____

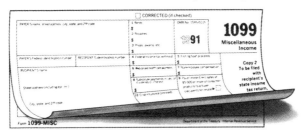

5

Congratulations, You're on Your Way!

*I*f all goes reasonably well at your temporary service interview, you can expect to be offered an assignment in the very near future. Temporary assignments can last for a day, a week, a month or longer. In general, a long-term assignment is considered anything extending for two weeks or more. Whatever your preferences, don't expect a long-term assignment at first. Most services will want to send you on a few short test runs to see how you do.

Naturally, the law of supply and demand will determine just how soon the service will have an available position for you to fill. The exact time frame will depend on the following factors:

■ *What Determines How Quickly You Will Be Sent on Assignment?*

- The temporary service's current inventory of available assignments
- The type of job skills you possess
- Your experience level
- Your salary requirements
- Your availability
- General economic conditions
- Regional economic conditions
- Your performance on the skills evaluations
- Your personnel coordinator's estimation of your appearance, attitude and ability to communicate

If you have flexible job requirements or skills that are in great demand, don't be at all surprised if you are offered an assignment on the spot. But, whenever that offer comes, you can expect your staffing manager to provide relevant information about the particular assignment. We suggest that you make sure each of the items on this checklist is covered *before* you accept any assignment:

■ *Seven Questions to Ask When an Assignment Is Offered*

1. How much does the assignment pay?
2. What kind of work will I be doing?
3. What business is the company in?
4. What is the dress code?
5. Can you provide me with exact directions?
6. To whom do I report?

7. What is the estimated length of the assignment?

Developing a Win-Win Relationship with Your Service

We believe that temping is a valuable opportunity for anyone willing to approach the experience with an open mind. Nevertheless, we have seen people get started on the wrong foot by adopting a negative attitude toward the entire process. There are any number of ways to express this negativity: poor dress, bad manners or a general lack of responsiveness or cooperation.

At times it is hard to say whether such negativity is due to an individual's overall lack of experience and professionalism or is simply an unfavorable response to the prospect of temping. If the latter is the case, we respectfully suggest that you may want to consider a workstyle option other than temporary employment. If, however, you are going to pursue temping for even a brief period of time, it will be to your benefit to put forth your best effort in terms of both attitude and actual work.

One way to enhance your chances for success is to develop a close working relationship with your personnel coordinator. As a rule, the beginning of any relationship is the time when rapport is developed and parameters are set. That's why it's in your best interest to start making your personnel coordinator an ally as soon as possible.

The best way to get on the right side of your personnel coordinator is to show her that you understand the delicate nature of her job. Once you are able to put yourself in this skilled professional's shoes, there will be a great deal you can do to make her life easier.

A key part of a personnel coordinator's function is to serve as a pivot point between the temporary employee, the temporary service and the service's client companies. That means the coordinator has to make a lot of people happy:

superiors at the temporary service, you—the temporary employee, and the corporate clients.

Each temporary employee sent out by a staffing manager is in effect an ambassador for the temporary service. The better you perform on assignment, the better your personnel coordinator—and the service—will look in the client's eyes.

If, on the other hand, you are unreliable, uncooperative or do unsatisfactory work, the personnel coordinator's judgment may be called into question. If the aberration is serious enough, the client might even choose another temporary service. But even a minor irregularity is likely to be noted for future reference.

Aside from your general professionalism and overall performance, you can endear yourself to your staffing manager by making yourself available to work on short notice and under less-than-ideal circumstances. These are some of the favors your staffing manager may ask you to do:

- Accept a lower rate of pay
- Accept an assignment that is far from home
- Accept an assignment in a field outside your area(s) of interest
- Accept an especially difficult assignment
- Accept an assignment during a time when you would rather not work
- Accept an assignment on short notice

At this point, many of you are probably wondering why you should put yourself out for someone you may hardly know. The answer harks back to the mutuality or win-win attitude that is so important in this business. Let's take a case in point.

Staffing managers are often called upon to provide temporary employees on short notice. If you are willing and able to pull your staffing manager out of a tight spot, she is likely to return the favor at a later date.

When Elizabeth registered with her service, she made it clear that she wanted to land a permanent job with an advertising agency or public relations firm. Since she was not particularly strapped for cash, she specified that she was only interested in high-paying data processing assignments for companies in those two categories.

Since Elizabeth started working for the service two months earlier, Jennifer, her staffing manager, had come through with the kinds of assignments she had requested. Elizabeth's latest assignment at a major advertising firm had ended the previous Friday. She had planned to take a week off before requesting a new assignment, but as yet unknown forces were conspiring to alter those plans.

It was 7 A.M. on the first Monday in months that Elizabeth had the luxury of sleeping in. She had just rolled over in bed when the phone rang. Elizabeth had put her answering machine on call screening the night before. Still, in her half-conscious state, she could hear a woman's voice imploring her to pick up the phone:

"Elizabeth, this is Jennifer. Please answer the phone if you're there. I need a big favor. It's very important!"

"Important to whom?" Elizabeth muttered to herself, as she clicked off call screening. "Hi, Jennifer," she yawned. "What's up?"

"I need someone for a three-day data processing assignment," Jennifer answered breathlessly. "It's at a financial services house, and I know that you're not really interested in that kind of assignment. Aside from that, the pay is a bit less than what I've gotten for you in the past. But the client is in the midst of an important project, and three people are out with the flu. I'd be much obliged if you could help me out on this one."

"Give me five minutes to get my bearings," Elizabeth responded, "and I'll call you right back."

Elizabeth quickly reviewed her options. She was certainly well within her rights to turn down this assignment. She and Jennifer had discussed her requirements on several occasions. Clearly, this assignment did not meet the conditions both of them had agreed upon.

On the other hand, Elizabeth recognized that this was an opportunity to do a favor for someone who might well be in a position to reciprocate down the line. It took her less than three minutes to return Jennifer's call.

"I've decided to accept the assignment," Elizabeth announced. "I know you're in a tight spot, and I'm glad to help you out. At the same time, I hope you'll keep me in mind when the kind of opportunity I'm looking for comes along."

"Absolutely," Jennifer responded, clearly grateful and relieved that her problem had been solved. "From this point on, you can consider yourself at the top of my list."

"That's great," said Elizabeth. "But I'm also aware that you have dealings with many different temps in the course of your busy schedule. I hope you won't think I'm being forward if I remind you from time to time that you owe me one."

"Certainly not," Jennifer replied. "I have no intention of forgetting this favor, although I understand why you might be concerned about getting lost in the shuffle. Believe me, you won't be sorry that you decided to get out of bed this morning."

As it turned out, Jennifer was good to her word. In the ensuing months, she came through with a number of desirable assignments, including one at the large public relations firm that offered Elizabeth the permanent position she has held for the past year and a half.

More than anything else, Elizabeth's experience is illustrative of the two-way street you can have with your service—if you play your cards right. We commend Elizabeth for demonstrating good judgment in the way she responded to Jennifer's request.

The question—*"important to whom?"*—that Elizabeth asked herself is one that would have occurred to most people. Why should you accommodate someone else's need and sacrifice your momentary comfort? It takes vision and good business sense to take the lead in demonstrating good will in any relationship. But, more often than not, it's well worth the relatively small risk.

By accepting a less desirable assignment, Elizabeth took a chance of being used by someone who might never have returned the favor. Certainly, there are such people in all businesses, including temporary services. Nevertheless, every good personnel coordinator we've ever met understands the principle of mutuality. In fact, the same can be said of virtually every successful person in any business.

"I recognized that this was an opportunity to do a favor for someone who could help me in my career," Elizabeth says in retrospect. "At the very least, it would have been shortsighted of me to pass up this chance. At worst, it might have been one of the stupidest mistakes of my professional life.

"That morning, I asked myself: What was my downside risk in accepting the assignment? The worst thing that could have happened was that Jennifer might never have returned the favor. Even so, what would I have lost—a few more hours of sleep or a few days off from work? It didn't take me long to decide that these were risks I could easily live with."

Understanding the principle of mutuality is at the heart of taking a win-win approach. In applying that principle, it is important to recognize your needs as well as the needs of the other person and then match them up. That's why we want you to keep in mind ten things your personnel coordinator wants and needs you to do.

▌ *Ten Ways You Can Help Your Personnel Coordinator Win*

1. Be easy to reach by phone.
2. Call in often or at the designated time when you are between assignments or otherwise hard to contact.

3. Make yourself available for calls during early mornings and late evenings.

4. Always show up to assignments on time.

5. Call as soon as possible if you are sick or otherwise unable to fulfill an assignment. Never just don't show up!

6. Always show up to assignments dressed appropriately.

7. Call when you are about to complete an assignment or if the completion date changes.

8. Call if you are asked to work overtime, offered a permanent position or if the nature of your assignment changes.

9. Make certain that you know exactly where and to whom you are supposed to report.

10. Take all complaints and grievances to your service—not to the client.

Now that you've seen some ways that you can help your personnel coordinator, consider some of the things she may be in a position to do for you.

▌ *Ten Ways Your Personnel Coordinator Can Help You Win*

1. Go out of her way to reach you when a desirable assignment comes in.

2. Call you for the highest-paying assignments in your skill area.

3. Find you assignments that are close to home.

4. Send you to companies that have reputations for being good places to work.

5. Try her best to meet your unique scheduling needs.

6. Make it a point to give you as much relevant information about your assignments beforehand as possible.
7. Send you on assignments that are of particular interest to you.
8. Send you on assignments that will enable you to expand your skills and improve your resumé.
9. Give you as much notice as possible with respect to when assignments will begin and end.
10. Respect your short- and long-term career objectives.

 ## What to Expect on the Job

As a rule, your service will take great care in matching you up with assignments. As noted earlier, your personnel coordinator should orient you as to the date and time the assignment is to commence, how to get to the job site, the company's dress code, where to report and the name of the supervisor to whom you should report. The client usually will have the work prepared for you in advance and a workplace ready for you. After all, it is in the client's interests that you have what you need to get down to business without costly delays.

Your supervisor should introduce you to the other team members and give you a brief tour of the facilities. Your personnel coordinator will usually tell you in advance about lunch hours and breaks. This information should be repeated by your supervisor upon your arrival. If it isn't, do not hesitate to ask.

The supervisor will apprise you as to company procedures and what you are expected to accomplish. Make sure you understand all instructions, and repeat them just to make sure.

Most supervisors want to do everything they can to make you productive. Of course, there are always exceptions. That's why it's a good idea to assume the initiative and find out what's expected of you. Take notes and make it clear that you are professional and well organized. And remember to show up at least fifteen minutes early on the first day of each new assignment. This will enable you to hit the ground running and start work on time.

When you arrive at a new assignment, introduce yourself to the supervisor and explain that you are a temporary from a particular service. Take the responsibility of learning how things are done at that company or department. If something isn't explained, don't be afraid to ask questions. Let the people around you know that you're resourceful and a problem solver.

Permanent staffers are usually told in advance that a new temp is coming on board. Because your presence is often indicative of a work overload or a personnel shortage, you can reasonably expect to be welcomed by your coworkers. Here again, there are always exceptions to the rule.

Depending on the corporate culture and the people in a particular department, a new temp might be greeted with a friendly, "Thank goodness you're here," or with an initial detachment. In any case, the wisest course of action is to take whatever comes in stride and remain focused on doing the best possible job. If you like your work environment, you can request long-term assignments at that company. If not, keep in mind that these situations are only temporary.

■ *Coping with Problems on the Job*

As in any situation, there are some problems that come up in temping. If you're lucky, you may never run into any of these difficulties. On the other hand, you may be unfortunate enough to encounter them all. Chances are you'll be hit with a few of these problems somewhere along the line. That's why we want to arm you with the problem-solving techniques you need to deal with each of them effectively.

You Can't Stand Your Job. Brenda, a bookkeeper, was assigned to a clothing manufacturer by her service. When she walked in, there was nobody to greet her. After sitting in the outer office for almost an hour, her supervisor appeared and curtly informed her that he was "in the middle of trying to put out a fire." Brenda would simply have to wait until he had a minute to deal with her.

When the supervisor finally reappeared, he showed Brenda to a desk that was piled high with work. Unfortunately, the supervisor was still in the midst of a crisis and much too busy to explain Brenda's responsibilities to her. He then proceeded to ask Florence, the bookkeeper at the next desk, to orient her. Instead of helping, Florence chose to ignore Brenda and proceeded to mutter some uncomplimentary things about temps.

By this point Brenda felt she had taken enough abuse. She had a strong impulse to simply walk off the job. She understood, however, that this is something that a professional temporary never does—no matter how bad the situation. One of the cardinal rules of temping is: *Once you have accepted an assignment, complete the day—at all costs!*

At her lunch break, Brenda called her assignment coordinator, Alex, from a pay phone and explained the situation. Alex proceeded to call the client and discuss the problem. Upon returning from lunch, Brenda's supervisor was waiting to apprise her of all her responsibilities.

The supervisor did not apologize or explain his earlier actions. But he at least made it possible for Brenda to fulfill her responsibilities. Meanwhile, over at the next desk, Florence remained as unfriendly as she was that morning. Still, Brenda was able to get through the day. Later that evening Brenda called Alex to discuss the situation further.

"Maybe I'm being oversensitive," she began. "But I'm the kind of person who likes to feel appreciated. I hate sitting next to someone who is obviously contemptuous of me and working for a supervisor who subjects me to such shabby treatment. I'd really appreciate it if you would find me another assignment."

Alex understood Brenda's predicament and appreciated the professional way she conducted herself. She had dealt with more than one temp who simply walked off a job and knew the problems such ill-advised actions could create.

No matter how bad things get, try to hang in for a few days so that your service can come up with a replacement. At the very least be sure to complete the day's work. Walking off an assignment reflects poorly on you and your temporary service.

Alex asked Brenda to finish out the week at the garment manufacturer, after which she promised to send her on an assignment with a client who had a good reputation for treating temporaries with consideration and respect. Brenda would have preferred being reassigned immediately. At the same time, she did not want to put Alex in a compromising position, so she agreed to finish out the week.

If you should ever find yourself on an assignment that you absolutely hate, we suggest that you follow Brenda's lead. Call your personnel supervisor at the first opportunity, and let her know that you are encountering problems on the job. While she's trying to work things out, continue to make an honest effort to do your job. This is a professional approach that can work to everyone's mutual benefit.

The personnel coordinator can speak with the client so that steps can be taken to rectify the situation. After all, it is not in a client's interests to have nonproductive temporaries on board. At the same time, it is in the temporary service's long-term interests to place people where they can be happy and productive.

By making your likes and dislikes known in a professional way, you give your personnel coordinator the opportunity to find you more suitable placements in the future. And again it's important to remember that, no matter how bad things get, these situations are only temporary!

There Seems to Be Little or Nothing to Do. Common sense dictates that a company would not go through the expense of hiring a temporary employee if there weren't sufficient work for that person to do. On occasion, however, this kind of problem does occur. Perhaps the department is undergoing some kind of momentary difficulty because of a change in management or a significant turnover in personnel. Whatever the reason, your responsibility is to deal with the problem in an intelligent, professional manner.

Some less industrious individuals might welcome this kind of situation. Imagine getting paid for doing little or nothing! Fortunately, most of the temporaries we work with have a far more responsible attitude. In general, they are interested in putting forth a good effort. In exchange they want to be respected and compensated fairly for their efforts.

If you should find yourself in a situation where there is little or nothing to do, speak to your supervisor. More often than not he will appreciate this feedback and take steps to rectify the situation.

Perhaps the work in the particular department to which you are assigned is not yet ready. If so, the supervisor may be able to use your efforts in another area. Should you be moved to a department other than the one to which you were assigned, make certain that the job description has not altered. If it has, be sure to contact your personnel supervisor as soon as possible.

If it turns out that the supervisor cannot provide you with sufficient work to keep you busy, you are still responsible for completing the assignment or, at very least, the day. In any case, be sure that you apprise your supervisor and personnel coordinator as to the nature of the situation.

A similar problem to the one described above involves boredom. Everybody has a different energy and motivational level, just as each person works at a different pace. On occasion you may find yourself on an assignment that is totally unchallenging, or on which you feel bored to tears. The situation may just be a bad match for which nobody can be faulted. If you are bored, you have a right to ask to be placed elsewhere. Your personnel coordinator will do her best, although she may ask you to complete your current assignment until a suitable replacement can be found.

There Is an Overwhelming Amount of Work to Do but not Nearly Enough Time to Complete It. If the temporary service has done its job and trained the client company on how to maximize the use of temps, you should not find yourself faced with an overwhelming amount of work when you arrive on the job site.

A good temporary service educates its clients as to the importance of assigning an appropriate amount of work to each temporary employee. Clients are also encouraged to have your work laid out and organized so that you can begin working immediately. But, here again, no temporary service can guarantee that things will always go as planned. In any case, there are a number of things you can do to rectify the situation.

It is up to you to introduce yourself to your supervisor and make sure that you have specific instructions telling you exactly how much work you are expected to accomplish and how the work is to be handled. By taking this simple step before you start, you can often pinpoint potential problems and correct them on the spot.

At other times, you may not recognize the problem until you get deeper into an assignment. If at any point you find that there is an overwhelming amount of work to do relative to a particular time frame, speak to your supervisor and ask him to prioritize the work for you. Don't make the mistake of waiting until the day is over to let your supervisor know there is a problem. Speak up as soon as you realize that the stated objectives you've been given are not accomplishable.

Your Assignment Turns Out to Be Substantially Different from the One You Were Sent to Do. Any temp who has walked into a new assignment only to find that she is expected to perform tasks that are completely different from those she was sent to do will tell you what a baffling and frustrating experience this can be. If this kind of thing should ever happen to you, we suggest that you retain your sense of proportion, as well as your sense of humor, as you proceed to take appropriate action.

Your first step is to call the mistake to the attention of the supervisor. The entire problem might have been caused by a clerical error, which can be corrected immediately. Should this turn out not to be the case, it is essential that you call your personnel coordinator immediately.

It is particularly important to inform your service of the mistake if the assignment you are being asked to do requires a higher skill level than the one for which you were hired. Such an assignment may require a higher billing rate to the client, which may also mean that you will be entitled to a higher pay rate.

There are a number of other factors that make it essential that you are performing only those tasks for which you've been hired. For one thing, you don't want to undertake assignments for which you lack the requisite skills. Doing so can make you—and your service—look bad to the client. In addition, performing certain kinds of work for which you are not trained can compromise your safety and that of your coworkers.

When a temporary service takes a job order from a client, a thorough job description should always be given. Among other things, that job description provides the basis for workers' compensation insurance coverage, as well as the client's bill rate and your pay rate. Since different kinds of work entail varying degrees of injury risk, it's essential that a service provide the appropriate coverage for each employee.

Remember, you are an employee of the temporary service that sends you on assignment—not of the client on whose premises the work is being performed. Therefore, you have an obligation to keep your service apprised of any change in your job description or function.

Another Temporary Doing the Same Kind of Work Is Earning a Substantially Higher Wage than You. A temporary employee who is working in the same department and doing the exact same kind of job may or may not be earning the same hourly wage as you. Although it's only natural to be curious about those around you, discussing your pay rate with others is not necessarily a good idea.

You should be aware that people don't always tell the truth about such matters. Before you take further action, you want to be reasonably sure the person giving you the information is honest.

There are reasons behind variances in pay rates that are not always obvious. Your more highly paid coworker may have a background or experience quite different from yours, and this is something that you can never know without asking.

Another temp's higher pay rate may be based on longevity with her service rather than on the current task she is performing. She may be working at an assignment that does not utilize her highest skill level, but the service may have chosen to pay her at the higher rate because she is a career temp with a long record of superior performance.

In some cases, it may simply be a question of supply and demand. Your coworker's temporary service may have had a problem filling the position and felt that it was in their best interests to keep the client happy. Consequently, they decided to send one of their more skilled temps out on a lesser assignment and pay her at a higher rate.

One key question to ask your coworker before jumping to any conclusion is: What temporary service are you working for? Not all services mark up each assignment at the same rate, so don't mistakenly conclude that your service is shortchanging you. If, however, the other temp works for the same service and has a comparable level of experience, you may want to discuss the matter with your personnel coordinator.

Even if the other temp does not work for the same service, you may want to have a talk with your assignment supervisor. Tell her that you are doing exactly the same job as someone else in your department and you would like to receive the same pay.

Depending on your particular situation and track record with the service, you may receive a higher pay rate for that particular assignment. Whether or not that increase will apply to subsequent assignments is something that will be decided on an individual basis.

Should you conclude that another temporary service is offering a higher rate of pay than the one for which you are currently working, you can always switch. Keep in mind, however, that there may be other people ahead of you at the new service for the kinds of positions you are seeking. Therefore, switching services is no guarantee that you will reach your goal. In any case, your hourly pay rate is only one aspect to consider when making your choice.

A Permanent Employee, Sensing that You Might Be Earning More than She Is, Asks You How Much You're Being Paid. This particular difficulty speaks to the increase in status temporary employees have enjoyed in recent years. In a growing number of instances, temporaries are earning a higher per-hour wage than permanent employees engaged in the same kind of work.

Here again, it is not a good idea to discuss your wages with anyone at the client company. In the first place, how much you earn is a confidential matter. Furthermore, comparing the way temporary and permanent employees are compensated is a little like comparing apples and oranges.

You may well be making a higher pay rate than a permanent employee. However, your permanent coworker will probably be receiving vacation time, pensions and other company benefits that are not part of your compensation. As we noted earlier, it is only human to be curious at times. Still, it's probably best to stay away from discussing pay rates— particularly with permanent employees. You have nothing to gain by entertaining such comparisons, and you risk incurring your coworker's resentment.

You Have the Solution to a Major Organizational Problem, but You're Not Going to Be Around Long Enough to Implement It. One of the reasons that the demand for temporary employees has been growing is that managers recognize the positive contributions these men and women are making to their companies. As a person who takes pride in what you do, it's natural to want to solve problems wherever you see them. Depending on the size and nature of the problem, your input may be welcome. On the other hand, it is important to recognize that, as a temporary, you are not on board to shake things up.

If you see that there is a major organizational problem, discuss the matter with your temporary personnel supervisor first. Many corporate managers are not particularly open to hearing about flaws and kinks in their operation. Sally found this out the hard way when she made what she considered to be a constructive suggestion to her department manager.

"Shortly after I first started temping, one of my first long-term assignments was as a computer programmer at a communications company," Sally recalls. "It didn't take me long to notice some major problems in the way some of their programs were set up. I proceeded to point these out to the manager of my department. He seemed taken aback by my criticism, but said he would look into it."

"The next day, my immediate supervisor called me aside and criticized me for violating protocol. He said, 'From now on, if you have any problems, bring them directly to me. Besides, you're not going to be here for that much longer. Who are you to tell us how to do things?'

"I felt horrible about being berated in this way. I was just trying to make a contribution. Later on I found out that the program I had criticized was one of the CEO's pet projects. Now I know that you have to be careful about stepping on people's toes.

"One of the reasons I love temping is that I am pretty much able to avoid corporate politics. But I found out that even temporaries are not immune. As you can imagine, that one incident made me far more circumspect about when and to whom I offer criticism and advice."

These days, if Sally has anything to say about a client's operations, she goes directly to her temporary assignment supervisor. That's exactly what you should do in such a situation.

If, in your personnel coordinator's professional opinion, the client is likely to be open to suggestions, she may ask you to put your thoughts in writing. Leave it to her to judge whether or not the necessary rapport exists to discuss critical suggestions with the client.

In any case, we strongly suggest that you do not take such decisions upon yourself. As Sally found out, it is not in your interests to ruffle feathers and cause strained relations. If your assignment supervisor does recommend that you put your suggestions in writing, make sure to frame them in a helpful rather than critical manner.

In the best of all possible scenarios, your assignment supervisor will raise these suggestions when he reviews your performance with the client. And who knows? Someone at that company may appreciate the fact that you were both concerned and bright enough to suggest an idea that could improve their business.

A Client Company Offers You a Higher Rate of Pay If You Join Them in Trying to Cut Your Service Out of Its Conversion Fee. It is unethical for you to accept a permanent position at a client company without first notifying the temporary service for which you are working. Keep in mind that the temporary service has gone to substantial expense to recruit you, orient you and place you. In some cases, they may have trained you in the very skills that are attractive to the client who seeks to hire you.

In addition to your own ethical standards, keep in mind that any client who tries to steal your services without compensating your temporary service is both unethical and in violation of a contract.

Uniforce asks each of its employees to complete a time-card—along with instructions for supplying correct information. This timecard is substantially the same as the ones used by other major temporary services.

After you fill out the timecard, the client signs at the bottom to verify that all the supplied information is correct. In addition, the client's signature constitutes an agreement to the terms and conditions on the back of each card. The first of these reads as follows:

"Uniforce incurs substantial recruiting, screening, administrative and marketing expenses in connection with the temporary employee ("Employee") named above. Client agrees that if Client hires Employee within 90 days after this date without agreement from Uniforce, Client will pay Uniforce a conversion charge."

The exact number of days and amount of the conversion charge may vary—depending on the service or the skill. In any case, the principle involved is the same. If a company is prone to pirating and breaking contracts, ask yourself how they are likely to treat you in the future. Are these the kinds of ethical standards with which you want to be associated? Do you want to entrust your future to a company that cannot be trusted?

As with so many other aspects of temping, the choice is yours!

6

Maximizing Your Money-Making Potential

As challenging and exciting as temping can be, we are well aware that the availability of skilled men and women would be scarce indeed if a paycheck weren't forthcoming at the end of a work week. Let's face it, most people need the money they earn to pay their bills. And those who don't actually need money still expect and want that paycheck.

It may be hard to fathom when you're struggling to make ends meet, but survival is not the main reason why people work. If it were, how could you account for the vast numbers of independently wealthy men and women who continue to get up every morning and put in an honest day's work?

The answer is simple: Most people need to have a place to go and some structured work to do. This basic need has been variously attributed to conditioning and to a work ethic that is at the foundation of human progress. Whatever the underlying reason, most people's self-esteem hinges at least partly on working and being compensated for those efforts. What's more, the type of job is not as much of a factor as you might think. Consider the following case in point.

Several years ago, a 44-year-old New Jersey watchman won a $5 million lottery. Afterwards, the gentleman declined all interviews. He respectfully asked for a little time to mull over the changes he might want to make in his life before talking to the press. Obviously, he no longer needed to work. Still, the statement this watchman made only a few short days after receiving his windfall is worth pondering.

"I'm going to keep on working at my present job," he told a large group of reporters. "I've got to get away from all this money."

Do you find this to be an unusual response? What would you do if a similar stroke of luck were to befall you? Take a permanent vacation from working? Go live on a tropical island? Perhaps. But before you make up your mind, we'd like you to take some time to think about the place money and work have in your system of values. The following questionnaire is designed to help you make that assessment:

▌ *Self-Evaluation Questionnaire: What Do Money and Work Mean to Me?*

1. The main purpose of money in my life is: (Please list in order of importance.)
   a. Freedom to choose when I work.
   b. Greater respect from family and friends.
   c. A more secure feeling about the future.
   d. More time for travel and leisure.
   e. To improve the way I see myself.

2. The most important reason I want to make more money is: (Please list in order of importance.)
   a. To buy material things.
   b. To help my family and friends.
   c. To improve my social standing.
   d. To feel better about myself.
   e. To have more freedom.

3. My primary motivation for working is: (Please list in priority order.)
   a. I need the money.
   b. I like having a place to go.
   c. I like being around other people.
   d. It makes me feel useful and needed.
   e. I need the structure an office provides.

4. A raise in pay at my job would indicate that:
   a. My boss or supervisor appreciates my value to the company.
   b. I'm better than those making less money than me.
   c. All my hard work is finally paying off.
   d. I've been underpaid all this time.
   e. I'm too good for this position.
   f. I'm capable of still better things.

5. My short-term financial objectives are: (Please list in priority order.)
   a. To make enough money to get out of debt.
   b. To make enough money to sustain my present lifestyle.
   c. To make enough money to improve my present lifestyle.
   d. To accumulate enough money to buy a particular possession.
   e. To accumulate enough money to take some time off from work.

6. My long-term financial objectives are: (Please list in priority order.)
   a. To be independently wealthy.
   b. To be financially secure.
   c. To always have enough money to get by.
   d. To have enough to retire comfortably.
   e. To have enough to help others.

7. If I had a sudden windfall of money, I would probably:
   a. Never work again.
   b. Take a long vacation, and then reconsider my options.
   c. Work at things I really enjoy, without regard to pay.
   d. Work at things I really enjoy—although what I was paid would still be just as important.
   e. Continue with the same workstyle and lifestyle I have now.

There is no grade or scoring formula for this questionnaire. Our main purpose in posing these questions is to stimulate you to think about the way your attitudes about money and work influence your career and life-style goals.

In case you were wondering, we are not trying to imply that temporary employment is as exciting as winning the lottery. Still, it does present you with a marvelous opportunity to experiment with a variety of workstyle and lifestyle options. But, again, the choices you make will depend on the goals that you set for yourself. And while there are certain limits and parameters, the amount of money you earn as a temp is, to a great extent, also a matter of choice.

Whatever your choices, we assume that each of you would like to make as much money as possible—all other things being equal. As you may have noticed, however, it is exceedingly rare for any given situation to be exactly the same as another. Instead, what you deal with in the real world are various kinds of trade-offs.

How much less money would you accept, for example, if everything else about a job was ideal? Say you had one job offer that paid half as much as another, but gave you the opportunity to work at something you genuinely cared about. Would you go for the fattest paycheck, or would the quality of the work be the most important variable?

Glen, a technical illustrator, was presented with just such a choice. Unfortunately it came at a time when he had been in the hospital and out of work for several months.

"It's strange how these things sometimes happen," Glen says reflectively. "I had only been looking for work for a week, when these two offers came through. One was for a small company that dealt with the kinds of projects that I love to work on. The other offer was from a much larger firm. The work was far less exciting, but the salary and benefits were substantially greater.

"My instinct was to take the more exciting position, despite all practical considerations. However, I was planning to get married in the near future. I guess that was the clincher, on top of all the economic hardships I had gone through recently. For better or worse, the timing of these two offers was such that I was hard pressed not to accept the higher-paying position."

As Glen learned, such choices can hinge more on a person's priorities and circumstances at the time than on his overall attitude toward work and money. That is why you can't ever be certain in advance of what option you would choose. Nevertheless, by increasing your understanding of the way you relate to money and work, you will be able to make informed decisions when you are faced with these choices.

 Estimating Your Value

Before you start evaluating how much you should be paid, it might be helpful to consider how and why different people are able to charge what they do. A glance at the classified ads in a recent edition of *The New York Times*

(August 16, 1992) demonstrates the wide variance in pay that men and women receive for different kinds of work:

Accountant (beginning, temporary)	$15 per hour
Administrative assistant	$22,000 per year
Computer network specialist	$78,000 per year
Dentist	$60,000 per year
Nurse	$33 per hour
Programmer/analyst	$1,000 per month
Receptionist	$17,000 per year
Teacher (substitute)	$54.00 per day
Telemarketer	$8.00 per hour
Word processor	$22.00 per hour

As vast as the above spread appears to be, it does not include the low or high ends of the payscale spectrum in our society. As you are doubtlessly aware, it is not unusual for professional athletes or Hollywood actors to make millions of dollars per year. On the other hand, the federal minimum wage at this writing is $4.25 per hour. How can such vast discrepancies in remuneration be justified? Let's look at this question in terms of some practical everyday dealings.

Have you ever wondered why a car mechanic charges $20 to $30 an hour for his services, while it is not uncommon for attorneys to charge $200 for that same hour's time?

In theory, the price one can charge for a particular service is supposed to be linked to supply and demand. But, in your experience, is it really ten times as difficult to find a qualified lawyer than it is to find someone who can competently repair your automobile? Probably not. How, then, do you account for a tenfold difference in pricing?

One of the underlying factors in determining what one can charge has to do with the public's perception of what things are worth. Think about it: Nobody would pay $200 an hour to get a car fixed. And, if an attorney asked for a mere $20 an hour, you'd probably question her capacity to represent you. This brings us back to the question at hand:

How Much Are Your Services Worth in Today's Temporary Job Market? The answer to that question depends on your skill level and work experience as well as on the pricing parameters that have been established for the kind of work you do. The good news is that the public perception of a temporary employee's value continues to improve. Consequently, many temps are now receiving a wage that is comparable to and even higher than that of permanent employees doing similar kinds of work. We expect this trend to become even more pervasive in the future.

When you try to estimate the value of your labors, keep in mind that you can only expect to be paid an amount that is within the established range for the particular kind of work you are qualified to do. If, for example, you are an experienced paralegal, you can expect to earn substantially more than if you are an entry-level typist. Assuming for a moment that this is the highest level at which the temp service can place you, there are still a number of things that can be done to increase your value.

As we've noted earlier, word processing has pretty much replaced typing in today's automated office. That's why a temp who is familiar with such popular software packages as WordPerfect or Microsoft Word will be in far greater demand—and worth more money—than someone with comparable typing skills who does not know word processing.

Most good temporary services offer free cross-training to employees in this and other potentially high-paying areas. Taking full advantage of such training opportunities is one way to increase your marketability and therefore your earnings potential.

We encourage you to compare carefully the different kinds of training options offered by the various temporary services, and give them the weight they deserve when deciding which service to go with. Here are some questions to ask a service in trying to determine the type and quality of training and cross-training programs they offer.

▌ Assessing Your Opportunities for Advancement

1. Exactly what kind of training and cross-training programs are available?

2. Are these programs free?

3. What skills and/or experience do I need to qualify?

4. Do I have to work for a specific number of hours before I am eligible for a particular course?

5. If I take advantage of a training opportunity, will I be required to make a commitment to work for the service in the future?

6. Is the training being offered in a skill that is in great demand?

7. Is the training done on a one-to-one basis, in a classroom or through self-teaching tutorials?

8. Are tuition reimbursements available for more formal training opportunities offered at local schools and colleges?

9. If so, how long do I have to work for the service before I am eligible?

10. Once I successfully complete a particular course of training, how much of a pay increase can I expect?

Betty is a 47-year-old homemaker who had been out of the work force for 18 years. Before she decided to devote herself to raising a family, Betty had been a secretary who was in great demand. Aside from having a professional attitude, she was highly regarded because of her typing speed and accuracy. During the intervening years, Betty had often helped retype term papers for her twin boys and had donated her skills to the PTA and other community groups.

When the twins reached their junior year in high school, Betty felt that there was no longer any need for her to spend so much time at home. Although her family was not hurting for money, Betty decided that the time had come, as she put it, "to get back out into the real world and see if I could find something interesting and meaningful to do.

"I could still type almost 90 words per minute, so I knew that I would be able to find some kind of job. But I saw that as a short-term objective. I had never touched a computer or word processor in my life, but I knew that this was the way for me to turn my existing skills into something that could lead to better things."

When Betty interviewed the various temporary services in her area, she made it clear that word processing and computer training were priorities.

"There were two services that offered me immediate typing assignments. One offered an hourly pay rate that was somewhat higher than the other. But the second company offered me far more extensive training opportunities, even though some of them would not be available until I worked for a certain number of hours. Still, I felt that it was in my interests to go with a service that recognized my potential and was willing to invest in it. That was worth far more to me than a slightly higher initial paycheck."

It took Betty only a few weeks to become familiar with WordPerfect. Jack, Betty's personnel coordinator, was impressed. He saw Betty as someone with whom his service could develop a mutually profitable relationship. Jack pointed out to Betty that versatility is an important factor in increasing the size of a temp's paycheck.

"I recall Jack saying: 'You know, Betty, a temp who is proficient at four or five word-processing packages is in a stronger position than someone who knows just one or two. You seem like a fast learner, so I'd like to assign you to companies where you'll have a chance to learn new programs.' Jack also helped me schedule some time for cross-training at the service."

By the end of the second month, Betty had almost doubled her initial salary. But this was only the beginning.

Because Betty took full advantage of the various cross-training programs offered by her service, she became proficient in three other popular word processors over the next six months. Betty has received several permanent job offers, but she has decided to stick with temping—at least for now.

"Learning to use a computer and mastering these different word processing programs has given me a tremendous feeling of accomplishment," she says enthusiastically. "I have complete confidence that I can learn any new software package in a short amount of time.

"When the right offer for a permanent job comes my way, I may eventually go for it. But, for now, I like having the flexibility to devote time to my family. Things have really worked out well. I'm especially happy that I decided to pass up a few extra bucks for a chance to get involved with a temp service that is committed to helping me realize my goals."

■ Tips for Maximizing Your Earnings

Like Betty, you can significantly increase your pay rate by taking full advantage of various training opportunities. It will, however, take some time for you to learn new skills, and you may need to earn more money right now. You can also ask your service for a raise at your present skill level. But, as you will see, this, too, may not be immediately forthcoming.

Now for the good news: No matter what your skill level or present negotiating position, there are a number of things you can do to earn more money with a temporary service:

- Let your assignment coordinator know that you want to work as much as possible and that you are flexible about the kinds of assignments you're willing to accept.

- If you find that you need more money than can be generated during the traditional 9-to-5 workday, make yourself available for evening and weekend work.

- Keep in mind that, in most states, you are legally entitled to overtime once you work 40 hours in any given week.

There may be times when a temporary service cannot provide you with the volume of work you request. Perhaps there has been a drop off in the demand for someone with your particular skills, or the service may be experiencing a slow period. If you feel that your service is not showing results in placing you, you can try your luck elsewhere.

Since your agreement with a temporary service is not exclusive, you are perfectly within your rights to sign up with two or more services—however many it takes to keep you working. Just be certain that you are honest about what you are doing and diligent in keeping your commitments. As a rule, your hourly pay and benefits tend to increase as you log more time with one service, so don't forget to factor that into your decision.

Before you start working for any temporary service, make sure to ask what its policy is with respect to hourly increases based on performance and longevity. When you reach these plateaus, make certain that the appropriate increments have been added to your paycheck. Don't count on your service to implement these raises automatically. Take it upon yourself to inform the service whenever you qualify for a raise or bonus.

Since your rate of pay can vary from assignment to assignment, don't forget to question what you will be receiving each time you start a new assignment. If you feel that the pay for a particular assignment is too low, ask your personnel coordinator if she has anything else for you or if she expects something better to materialize in the near future.

If You Don't Think You're Getting What You're Worth, Do Something about It! It's only natural to become upset if you feel that you're being underpaid. But, remember, the type of assignments that your service will seek for you depends primarily on its current assessment of your skills.

In general, the more your temporary service can demand for your skills, the more money you—and it—will be paid. It is, therefore, in a service's best interests to place you in assignments that utilize your highest skill level. At the same time, it is your responsibility to make certain that your service has accurately assessed your skills.

If you feel that your performance on the skill evaluations does not present a true picture of what you can do, discuss the matter with your assignment coordinator. If you have recently upgraded your skills in a particular area, ask to be retested immediately. If, after taking those steps, you still feel that you are not being offered assignments that utilize your highest skill level, you might want to try another temporary service. There are, however, two things we want you to keep in mind:

1. You may have to accept a lesser assignment or rate of pay until a service is convinced that you have upgraded your skills.

2. No service can guarantee that it will always be able to place you on assignments that utilize your best and most price-worthy skills.

If you want to get a general sense of the present value of your skills, you can call other services and check the current classified ads in your local newspaper. You might also speak to other temps and ask what they are earning.

In assessing how much is being paid for the kind of work you do, keep in mind that the upper range of a quoted or advertised or hourly rate is likely to be available only to the most experienced and proven people. Therefore, when you see an ad for word processors that gives a pay range of $15 to $25 an hour, common sense should tell you that the high-end dollars are meant for those temps a service considers the cream of the crop.

▌ *How a Temporary Service Evaluates Your Worth*

Temporary services view a person's demonstrated skills in an interview situation as just the beginning of the story. Consequently, you can expect your assignment coordinator to keep tabs on how you are doing on the job. Assuming you intend to make a positive contribution wherever you go, you should welcome these follow-up inquiries. All services will periodically call your job supervisor in order to assess your performance. In some cases, written evaluations may be requested as well. It is in your interest to have any positive remarks regarding your job performance put down in writing.

If, for example, your supervisor compliments you for a job well done, ask if he would consider writing you a short note to that effect. When you complete the assignment, ask for a letter of recommendation. This will be useful when you want to negotiate a pay increase at your present service or establish your value with a new service. Such complimentary letters will also be helpful if you should decide to apply for a permanent position.

As we noted in Chapter Four, there are times when temporary employees encounter difficulties on the job. If you feel that there is a problem not of your own making, make sure to keep your personnel coordinator apprised. It is also a good idea to keep a written diary or at least the kind of evaluation form illustrated on page 92. If your service declines to give you a pay raise because of a poor performance evaluation, such documentation can help support your side of the story.

No matter what the job situation, a certain number of misunderstandings are inevitable. In some instances the fault may lie with the client company.

A word processor assigned to work on a particular piece of software finds that he is expected to use another software package on which he is not as proficient. As a result, he receives a poor evaluation. Obviously this problem is not the fault of the temporary employee. Designating the specific skills necessary for a given assignment is the responsibility of the client company.

There are also times when misunderstandings or problems can be traced to the temporary service. If a personnel coordinator does not do a thorough job of interviewing or evaluating an employee's skills, for example, she may send that person out on an inappropriate assignment. A good service will take great care to avoid such mistakes, but they do happen on occasion.

At Uniforce, we value our employees' opinions and feedback. That's why we encourage them to periodically evaluate us, as well as our clients. We accomplish this by asking our temporaries to complete a simple evaluative questionnaire, which we call "You're a Star with Uniforce." Evaluations are sought with respect to the following:

- Accuracy of the job description
- Working conditions
- Treatment on the job
- Overall impression of the job
- Any other comments

If the questionnaire you complete contains any negative comments, someone from the service will call you to investigate. Perhaps you indicated that the equipment on which you were asked to work was in bad repair or the job description you were given was inaccurate or incomplete. If the problem is with the client, someone from the service will call and tactfully make constructive suggestions. If the source of the misunderstanding is traced to the temporary service, appropriate steps will be taken to avoid future repetition.

Here again, we see an example of the mutually positive and reciprocal relationship forward-looking services seek to develop with their employees. Just as we solicit your impressions and opinions of us and our clients, we are diligent in our ongoing efforts to obtain detailed and accurate information about you. Most good services take great care in placing employees and orienting corporate clients. In most instances, all goes well and the reports are largely positive. However, there are exceptions.

When a personnel coordinator receives an unfavorable evaluation, she will attempt to pinpoint the source of the problem. If this should happen to you, be prepared to support your side of the story. Most temp services will make an honest effort to find out where the fault lies. If a service concludes that a problem is the employee's responsibility, that person will be replaced immediately.

In most cases, an employee will be given a second chance, although performance will be closely monitored for a period of time. If a service receives a second negative evaluation, it is not likely to go on placing that person in the future. No service can afford to reassign temps who continue to receive poor evaluations or who have problems while on assignment.

In a surprising number of cases, negative evaluations are the result of a lack of reliability or professionalism, rather than a deficiency in a person's skills. No matter how proficient you are at what you do, a positive attitude and good work habits are always important factors in developing a good track record with your service and its client companies. In most cases, the effort you put into these aspects of your presentation will translate into more money in your weekly paycheck.

 Asking for a Raise

Most temps who do the same kind of work for a service for six months or more can expect to begin receiving some kind of pay increase—assuming they have received *excellent* reports from client companies. On the other hand, a mere passing grade is not going to give you much ammunition when you try to negotiate a raise.

A temporary service is far more likely to reward employees who receive rave reviews for their performance than those who just show up and do passable work. This same principle is true in most industries: Average people are not hard to come by; exceptional people are highly coveted and treated accordingly.

If you feel that you are truly deserving, you should not be shy about asking for a raise. Before you start negotiating, however, make sure you've taken the steps we suggested earlier in this chapter: Check the classified ads to ascertain the going rate for the kind of work you do. Call several other temporary services and ask them to give you a ballpark figure of what they are paying people with comparable skills to yours.

Most services will try to be fair with you. At times they may overlook the fact that a pay increase is warranted. On other occasions, they may simply not bother offering you a raise until you take the initiative of coming in and bringing the matter to their attention.

Again, we encourage you to assert yourself in asking for what you feel you deserve. Just be prepared to support your contention that an increase is warranted at that particular time. Please keep in mind that, irrespective of your skill level or past performance, the rate of pay you receive is subject to change from one assignment to the next.

Your assignment coordinator's decision about whether or not to give you a raise will be based largely on her assessment of your immediate and long-term value to the service. The following questionnaire lists ten of the criteria a coordinator is likely to use in making that determination. Put a check in the space provided to the right of each statement that applies to you. If you can honestly mark off at least eight out of ten, you may well have grounds for answering *yes* to the question: Do you deserve a raise?

▌ Questionnaire: Do You Deserve a Pay Raise?

1. You've accepted most assignments offered by the service.

2. You've worked for the service on a regular basis for six months or more.

3. You consistently receive excellent evaluations.

4. You have maintained an outstanding attendance record.

5. Client companies frequently ask that you be reassigned to them.

6. You've been cited for displaying a positive, professional attitude.

7. You've helped your service when they were in a pinch on at least one occasion.

8. You've never had a problem on an assignment for which you were deemed to be at fault.

9. You've upgraded your skills since starting to work with the service.

10. Your current rate of pay is not on par with what other employees with comparable skills and experience are earning.

▌ Receiving Benefits from Your Temporary Service

The issue of such job benefits as medical insurance, paid vacations and pensions has become a growing concern for the temporary services industry. As we have noted, an increasing number of temporaries are now paid on a par with permanent employees in terms of base salary. When it comes to benefits, however, the formula is somewhat different.

Traditionally, when a person went to work for a company on a permanent basis, he or she was expected to render loyal service for a number of years. In return that individual received a comprehensive benefits package that included such things as medical insurance, a dental plan, paid vacations, pensions and profit sharing.

In contrast, a person who elected to work as a temporary often was not particularly concerned with such perks. Freedom and flexibility were the main benefits sought by most temps. While these are still among the main attractions of the temporary workstyle, benefits are becoming increasingly important to everyone connected with the temporary services industry.

A survey by the National Association of Temporary Services indicates that concerns about benefits are now very important to temporary employees.[1] This has come about in part because of the general upward mobility of the temporary services industry.

In previous decades, many temps had spouses whose full-time jobs provided medical coverage for the entire family. Almost half of all temporary employees now provide the main source of income for their households.[2] Therefore, it is far more likely that these are the family members who will be counted on to furnish medical insurance.

Steve had been a CPA with the same accounting firm for seven years. Since he was laid off two years earlier, he has been working regularly on a temporary basis. As far as Steve is concerned, the only downside he can see to this workstyle relates to medical insurance and other benefits.

"I never thought I would be so happy working temporary," Steve admits. "But I really enjoy the challenge of coming into a new company and solving its problems. For the most part, the salary I've been receiving is more than what I was earning at my permanent job. I am somewhat concerned, though, about medical and dental coverage for myself and my family.

"The corporation I worked for had an extremely comprehensive plan. At some point, my son needed surgery, and the entire procedure was almost totally covered. The same was true when my wife required a lengthy hospital stay. Now I have to contribute hundreds of dollars each month to a group plan, and it still doesn't match the coverage I had on my job.

"The added expense of medical costs is something I have to factor into comparing my temporary and permanent job situations. So far things are working out well. Frankly, I'm not even in the market for a permanent position. But, if I ever do decide to go that route, medical insurance and other benefits will be the reason."

Anything that is of great concern to temporary employees must ultimately be addressed by the services for which they work. Good people in the labor market know what they are worth, and temporary employees are no exception. That's why any service that wants to remain competitive must now provide a range of benefits to its employees.

Corporate America has come to understand how important temporary employees are to its long-term profitability. Consequently, corporations want their temps to be motivated on a par with permanent employees. In recent years corporate clients have been exerting pressure on temporary services to improve the range and quality of benefits they offer. For the most part, the industry has responded to these concerns.

Temporaries who work for one service for a significant time period can expect to earn excellent vacation and holiday plans. Many of the better services offer a variety of medical programs. As your tenure with a service increases, so will the benefits for which you will be eligible.

It is important that you understand the options and limitations of the various benefits plans offered by temporary services. Otherwise, you may develop unrealistic expectations. That said, we can frankly advise you not to expect much in the way of pensions and retirement programs.[3] Some industry analysts expect this situation to improve in the future. However, if you are someone who places a great value on such benefits, we suggest that you develop the kind of temporary-employment game plan that will lead to a permanent position.

Those of you who continue to establish yourself with a service can expect the variety and quality of benefits to increase proportionately. Uniforce currently offers 128 different benefits, discounts and bonuses for our temporary employees. These include:

- Vacation pay
- Holiday pay
- Temporary or interim medical insurance
- Discount dental and prescription drug plans
- Free skills upgrading
- Performance bonuses
- Talent scout referral bonuses and salary incentives
- Tuition reimbursement
- Travel and hotel discounts

Although each temporary service differs in terms of type of benefits offered and eligibility requirements, we think it will be instructive for you to see how the major services handle some of these matters.

Vacation Pay.   As with most benefits, you probably will not be entitled to any paid vacation time for working on one or two short-term temporary assignments. However, you will be able to get vacation and holiday pay from some temporary services if you put in the required amount of time.

At most Uniforce offices, vacation pay may be earned at the rate of 2½ days extra for every 750 hours worked in a consecutive six-month period. A second option allows a temp to accumulate 1,400 hours over a consecutive 12-month period and receive a full five days' vacation pay.

Holiday Pay. A temporary employee has the option of being paid for six national holidays: Christmas, New Year's Day, Thanksgiving, Memorial Day, Independence Day, and Labor Day. In order to be eligible, an employee must work 800 hours in a 12-month period prior to the holiday. In addition, he or she must work the week before and the week after the holiday.

Permanent Major Medical Insurance. Temporary services offer varying degrees of medical coverage. This is often contingent on an employee's skill level and tenure with the service.

It is difficult to provide continuous medical coverage to temps who do not work continuously. Many temps work only part of the time, perhaps only a few months out of the year. In general, most services offer their temps the opportunity to sign up with a group insurance plan. Depending on how many hours an employee puts in, she may be required to pay all or part of the premium.

Temporary or Interim Medical Insurance. Some services now offer temporary or interim medical insurance. People who are between jobs and want to be covered immediately are eligible. Such individuals are offered a group plan at a group rate with no waiting period requirement. Until they put in a specified number of hours, however, these individuals are generally required to pay for all or most of their coverage.

Free Skills Upgrading. Employees who want to upgrade their existing skills can make an appointment to come to the temporary service office and use the available equipment or go through the various training programs. Most services encourage skills upgrading. However, it is important to contact your office in advance to make sure that space and equipment will be available.

Performance Bonuses. These are paid incentives offered by many services to encourage temporaries to work more hours and to stay with the service. After people log a certain number of hours during a three-month period, they are paid a cash bonus. These bonuses can be earned for each three-month period where the hourly requirement is met.

Talent Scout Referral Bonuses and Salary Incentives. Any time you refer a skilled temporary to a service, you can expect to receive a cash bonus once the referred person has successfully completed her first assignment. The actual amount of these bonuses vary according to the person's skill level as well as the policy of the temporary service.

In the Uniforce system, each individual franchisee decides how much it will pay for referring skilled people to its office. For instance, you may receive $50 for referring a person who has experience on a Macintosh computer or $25 for referring a person who is proficient at WordPerfect. The referral or talent scout bonuses usually don't exceed $100 for office jobs. They can, however, be significantly higher in professional areas that are in great demand, such as is currently the case with registered nurses.

Tuition Reimbursement. Employees may be eligible for such repayment after they have worked a minimum number of hours. Reimbursement is generally handled with a three-part payment plan: One-third of the tuition is reimbursed after a person has worked 100 hours, one-third after the next 100 hours and the final third after the next 100 hours. This benefit is one that is designed to attract and retain proven career temps.

■ *Your Rights as a Temporary Employee*

As noted earlier, as long as you are accepting assignments through a temporary service, it is your employer of record. Therefore, it is the service's responsibility to provide workers' compensation insurance and to make all mandatory deductions as prescribed by both state and federal law. This includes taxes and social security—as well as the employer's share of unemployment insurance. Temporary services must abide by the same laws as other employers with respect to minimum wages and overtime. Be aware that when you work as a temp, you have the same legal and civil rights as any other employee. That means that you cannot be discriminated against because of your race, religion, sex, age or national origin—in terms of both hiring and compensation. You also cannot be discriminated against because of a physical handicap, pregnancy, childbirth or related medical conditions.

Should you encounter problems in these areas, the following federal agencies may be of assistance:[4]

> The Equal Employment Opportunity
> Commission (EEO)
> 2401 E Street N.W.
> Washington, DC 20507
>
> The U.S. Department of Labor
> 200 Constitution Avenue N.W.
> Washington DC 20210

▋ *Notes*

1. NATS Survey, *Contemporary Times*, Winter 1990.

2. *Ibid.*

3. Any employee not covered by a company pension plan may be eligible for an Individual Retirement Plan (IRA). Consult with your tax advisor for more information.

4. Please note that all states have their own EEOs and Departments of Labor. In addition, the EEO maintains 22 district offices in large cities throughout the country, as well as 26 smaller area offices.

7

*F*orever Temporary!

*A*s a significant segment of society gradually moves away from the rigid confines of the traditional 9-to-5 work week and places a greater emphasis on time spent with family and leisure activities, temporary employment is proving to be a permanent solution for a growing number of women and men. An estimated one-third of all Uniforce employees become career temps. These individuals thrive on the lifestyle opportunities afforded by the temp workstyle. Career temps enjoy meeting new people and are stimulated by the challenge of succeeding in different work environments. Some of these men and women start out with the idea that they will work their way into a permanent position. But, inevitably, they remain temps.

If you're looking for diversity, adventure and exposure to a variety of people and challenging work environments, then career temping is a road you may want to travel.

- Do you value independence?
- Do you hate bureaucracies and corporate politics?
- Do you want to devote more time and energy to your family?
- Do you like to travel?
- Do you want to spend more of your time involved in leisure and creative activities?
- Do you want to attain a balanced lifestyle that does not revolve solely around your career?

If you answered "yes" to at least two of the above questions, career temping is an option you may want to consider.

Most career temps are people who, for a variety of reasons, prefer not being tied down to a permanent job. While some career temps do prefer working for one client company on a continual basis, their psychic needs are quite different than those of people who thrive on being permanent employees.

It's important to recognize that, while you may be earning a comparable salary and doing comparable work to someone employed on a permanent basis, working as a career temp requires a different mind-set. If you're after the kind of job security that has been traditionally associated with working for a single company for your entire career, we suggest that you think of temping as a means to an end rather than a career objective. We will be exploring this option in Chapter Eight.

In general, career temps are not interested in climbing the corporate ladder, nor do they have a yen for the fast track.

A growing number of career temps are more committed to their families than to their careers. Others are free spirits who like to travel and enjoy having the option of working only when they want to work.

Career temps do not come from any particular skill category. Some are word processors. Others are legal secretaries. Still others are engineers, lab technicians or nurses. Most people become career temps because of their lifestyle and workstyle preferences, not their level of education or the particular skills they bring to the workplace.

The vast majority of career temps are well educated. According to the National Association of Temporary Services, 82 percent of all temporary employees have more than a high school education. Most attended college, with 31 percent receiving degrees and 5 percent holding advanced degrees.[1]

Perhaps some of you are wondering if there isn't a contradiction in the idea of being a permanent temporary. We are indeed talking about a relatively new phenomenon. In fact, becoming a career temporary was something that could not have even been imagined twenty—or even ten—years ago. But as we approach the twenty-first century, career temping is an option that more and more people are taking advantage of.

Is Career Temping for You?

Ultimately, the decision to carve out a career in temporary employment will entail taking a complete inventory of such factors as finances, family obligations, lifestyle requirements and the importance of fringe benefits. Still, your needs, desires and personal preferences are issues that should never be relegated to a back seat.

For the most part, we find that women and men who choose temping as a career have the following workstyle and lifestyle preferences.

▌ *Profile of the Career Temporary*

- Career temps require more freedom and flexibility. They do not like being hemmed in by a conventional job.

- The career temp may wish to work on an ongoing basis but does not want to be tied down to the same daily routine at one place.

- Career temps enjoy being free of the pressures and politics that go along with a permanent appointment.

- The career temp may want to work a few months a year or only on certain days or during selected seasons.

Four key advantages that attract women and men to the career-temp option are shown below. Let's explore the role each of these issues plays in how you formulate your work-style and lifestyle objectives?

▌ *Benefits of Career Temping*

1. Flexibility
2. Freedom
3. Choice
4. Control

▌ *Flexibility and Family vs. the Fast Track*

"There's a stirring in the hearts of many baby boomers reassessing priorities, questioning the sacrifices that are often required in terms of family life by unbridled careerism."[2]

Lucy had built a successful career as a claims manager for a large insurance company. During the course of her nine years with that organization, 36-year-old Lucy had taken two short, unpaid childcare leaves to give birth to her two children. Other than that, she had hardly ever missed a day's work. In fact, Lucy was an admitted workaholic who sometimes put in a 70-hour workweek.

"It had taken a long time for me to attain a managerial position with my company," Lucy recalls. "Eighteen months after receiving that key promotion, I became pregnant with my first child. Naturally I was happy, but I also worried about how this turn of events would impact my career.

"I had originally planned to continue working until right before my due date. Then I hoped to return to work a few weeks after delivering my baby. Unfortunately, I had some physical problems during the eighth month and was forced to take an unpaid leave.

"After my son Billy was born, I felt physically spent and needed some additional rest. Nevertheless, I returned to work six weeks later, despite my doctor's advice and my husband's wishes. I loved my baby, but I obsessed about not advancing any further on my job if I stayed out too long.

"My second pregnancy, which came three years later, was unplanned. This time my doctor insisted that I stop working during my seventh month and stay home for at least three more months before returning to work. I felt that I had just started getting back on track with my career and now I was getting derailed again. I wasn't aware of it then, but now I see how much joy I missed out on because I was so concerned about career advancement.

"I wound up staying home for 15 weeks after my daughter Andrea was born. Frankly, I was a nervous wreck by the time I returned to work. Nearly five years had passed, and I hadn't received a promotion or a substantial raise. I really felt like a failure, and I guess these negative feelings started seeping into my family life.

"My husband and I began fighting more than we ever had. Andrea, who was a more difficult baby than my first, seemed to have problems adjusting to daycare. Eventually, my husband and I went for family counseling, and I soon came to realize that my priorities needed to be rearranged."

After nine years on the job, Lucy gave notice that she was quitting. She then spent the next three years as a full-time homemaker. During that time, her family life became richer than she had ever imagined. By then, both children were attending school and adjusting extremely well.

"I felt it was time to go back to work," Lucy recalls. "But I had no intention of making the same mistake I made before. When a friend told me about the workstyle options available in temporary employment, I investigated. It now appears that I've made temping a career choice."

In the course of her tenure as a temp, Lucy has become a banking specialist. Her evaluations are consistently excellent, and financial institutions request her back on a regular basis. Lucy has been offered a number of permanent positions, but she chooses to remain a career temp.

"I sometimes can't believe that I've turned down the kind of prestigious, high-paying positions I would have killed for at another time in my life. I guess you can say that my outlook has changed dramatically!"

Lucy is typical of a lot of people of her generation who placed too much emphasis on having a high-powered career. Like many of her peers, she has made a complete 180-degree turnaround in her thinking about what gives her real satisfaction in life and where her priorities lie.

"If I were asked to choose between my family and my career, there would be no choice. But the great thing is, I don't have to choose. Career temping has made it possible for me to enjoy work and a rich family life."

Lucy's change in priorities is typical of the shifting values of the 1990's. There is growing evidence that mothers and fathers are now willing to make far greater sacrifices in order to spend more time with their families.

In a poll of 1,000 career professionals, 82 percent of the women said they would choose a career path with flexible full-time hours and more family time but slower career advancement over a fast-track career without adaptable hours.[3]

In case you think that women are the only ones whose values are changing, consider the following:

A survey conducted by the DuPont Corporation revealed that 56 percent of male employees favored adjustable schedules that provided more family time, and 40 percent would consider working for another employer who offered more job flexibility.[4]

The so-called men's movement, which came to prominence in the 1990's, has made a growing number of men painfully aware that there is something missing from their emotional lives. Robert Bly and others attribute this void in part to the fact that work in the post-industrialized society no longer has any intrinsic value that a father can share with his son.

In earlier times, a farmer or craftsman took his son to the fields or the shop and taught him not only a trade but also the meaning of manhood. But in the second half of the twentieth century, many work-absorbed fathers went to the office or factory and were rewarded only with a paycheck. These emotionally drained men had little time and energy to give their sons.[5]

Many of the boys who grew up in the shadow of this emotional void are now themselves fathers who are willing to go to great lengths not to inflict the same kind of pain on their own sons and daughters.

"Many parents who have overworked in recent years now want to change," Patricia Aburdene and John Naisbitt remark in Megatrends for Women:

"[Taking] time off work to spend time with family is emerging as the status symbol of the 1990's . . . Many people would trade a day's pay for a day off . . . Corporations that recognize [this] need . . . and how much it improves people's work will attract the best people and improve productivity."[6]

Committed temporary service professionals are in the business of creating adaptable workstyles for their people.

We anticipate that, in the coming years, this will become an even more important aspect of what we do.

Futurist Carolyn Corbin, who authored the book *Strategies 2000*, believes that emphasis on career and corporate loyalty will continue to decrease—particularly among baby boomers who currently account for over 50 percent of the work force.

"Baby boomers who were once workaholics have come to realize that there are more important things in life. These men and women, who are now in their thirties and forties, have always been self-dependent and oriented toward self-fulfillment. As more of them face the demands of child-rearing, total devotion to careers and jobs is declining. Money and career advancement are still important issues, but quality time spent with families and pursuing other interests is now perceived as being more critical."[7]

▌ *Let Your Spirit Fly!*

Jeannie has been temping for the past six years. During that time, she has been fulfilling her dream of traveling to different parts of the country. Although she has full-charge bookkeeping skills, Jeannie has also accepted a number of data processing and telemarketing assignments.

"For me, seeing new and exciting places is a priority," says Jeannie. "I'm not independently wealthy, so I need to work in order to support myself. With Uniforce's *Get Up and Go* program, my dream is being realized. Whenever I want to go to a new city, I simply tell my personnel coordinator, and she forwards my records to the nearest Uniforce office.

"When I am able to give enough notice, my service almost always comes through with a high-paying assignment in my field. At other times I've had to accept lower-paying positions in areas that did not utilize my highest skill level. Still, it's a great feeling to know that there's always a job waiting for me in each new city. And, for the most part, the variety of assignments has been both challenging and enjoyable."

Elaine, who works out of our Bloomington, Minnesota, office, is an excellent word processor. Since starting to temp in 1988, Elaine has developed skills in three word processing packages. For the past five years, Elaine has worked pretty much on a consistent basis. Why, then, you might ask, does she continue to turn down permanent positions? We'll let Elaine answer that question:

"Even though I sometimes work a 40-hour week, I like knowing that I can take time off whenever I want. My husband and I have a large network of friends and we enjoy hosting out-of-town guests in our spacious home.

"I recently took up painting, and I enjoy going out into the woods on a sunny afternoon to capture the light. I'm also a pretty fair golfer. Lately a group of my friends have started playing regularly on Tuesdays, so I've told my personnel coordinator not to assign me on those days—at least for now."

Lily, who works out of our Melville, Long Island, office, has been temping since 1979. Her husband's executive position with an airline allows for frequent business and leisure travel. When Lily started temping, she was sent on general clerical assignments. As her skills improved, Lily was upgraded—first to figure clerk, then to accounting clerk and statistical typist.

On one of her recent assignments, Lily learned to use a popular financial software package. This valued skill, along with her positive attitude and good work habits, has made Lily one of her office's most in-demand temps. Lily has been offered several permanent positions, but has no interest in anything but career temping.

"I love learning new skills and being requested back at the companies I work for, but there's no way I would ever tie myself down to one job. My husband receives an extensive benefits package, so that is not a concern of mine. What I want is a way to earn extra money, while keeping my options open. I also enjoy the challenge of meeting new people and learning new skills. Temping has given me all those things."

Lily, Elaine and Jeannie are members of our *Careertemp Club*, an association whose membership has grown dramatically in the 1990's. As the need for balance replaces unbridled consumerism and careerism as a motivating force in people's lives, we expect this trend to continue indefinitely.

Here's why the better services go out of their way to make career temps feel like the special people they know they are:

- Career temps have established themselves in terms of both reliability and skill level and are, therefore, likely to be requested and called back by corporate clients.

- Career temps continue to generate income for a service over an extended period.

The more career temporaries a service can attract, the better it will be able to serve its corporate clients. Consequently, most temporary services offer additional benefits, training opportunities, bonuses and top assignments to individuals who are established or potential career temps.

At Uniforce we take great pride in our *Careertemp Club* and the advantages it provides. Aside from the perks we offer our career temps, we find that the following are the things our people most often cite when we ask them what they love most about temping as a career:

- I love meeting new people, and making new friends.

- I love going to new places, and being exposed to different industries.

- I love learning new skills—career temping is a constant learning experience.

- I love never having to deal with boring daily routines.

- I love never having to be stuck on a dead-end job.

■ Career Temping Your Way to a Balanced Lifestyle

"Many Americans now value time as highly as money," the authors of *Megatrends For Women* observe.[8] As we've seen, career temps use their time in many ways—to enrich their family lives, to pursue creative ventures, to travel or simply to relax. What about you? Does your use of time reflect your overall lifestyle priorities?

If you conceive of time as a kind of blank canvas upon which you create your days, you will realize that you can turn that canvas into almost anything you want. Try thinking of each action you take as a single brushstroke. If you add up all the brushstrokes you make each day, week and year, this will determine what your painting ultimately looks like.[9]

The paintings you create on your canvas reflect the objectives that you set for yourself. If, for example, you decide that money and a powerful career are the most important things in your life, your painting will look a lot different from one created by a person whose priorities are a rich family life or a desire to travel.

Most of us spend our time trying to attain success or self-fulfillment. But these, too, are subjective concepts that are linked to the way we set our priorities—and to the paintings we, as time artists, create on our canvases.

Our individual and collective value systems have undergone some radical changes over the past few decades. Consider the findings of a UCLA researcher who tracked the "life goals" of a quarter of a million full-time college students over a 25-year period.

In the early 1970's, the number one concern of students was "developing a meaningful philosophy of life." By 1989, in the wake of the "me decade," that value had dropped all the way down to ninth. Not surprisingly, "being well off financially" had taken over the number-one spot.[10]

The 1990's are often characterized as a decade in which

people are once again beginning to cherish the more human-istic and intrinsic values that were associated with the 1960's and early 1970's. Consequently, there seems to be a shift from being achievement oriented to finding one's sense of identity and fulfillment in non-work-related activities. To a great extent, this shift in values can be attributed to the need most people have to maintain balance in their lives.

If you spend years obsessed with making money and building a lucrative career, you are likely to find that other aspects of your life have been neglected. Futurist Carolyn Corbin believes that a person's ability to address his or her shifting need for balance is "an overriding lifeskill that is necessary for attaining any goal.

"It's ironic, but many people don't ever think about the need for harmony until things fall completely out of balance and they are faced with some kind of crisis. There are a number of issues and dimensions in our lives that must be kept in balance. These include finances and career as well as social, spiritual, emotional and physical health. If any one of these dimensions is neglected or given too much emphasis, our entire lives can be thrown into chaos.

"If, for example, you completely ignore your health and personal life for the sake of your career, this imbalance may cause you to eventually develop stress-related problems that prevent you from working.

"At that point you may find yourself in financial diffi-culty. And if, on top of that, you are dealt a wild card—say the unexpected illness of a family member—you will have allowed a lack of balance to render you vulnerable and ill equipped to cope with change and adversity."[11]

Before you can attain a healthy balance in your life, it's important to define your objectives. We often hear people talk about being a success. But what does that really mean—a fulfilling career, financial security, emotional and spiritual happiness, vibrant health, a rich family life? As we see it, truly successful people manage to achieve a harmonious balance of all these components.

▌ *Questionaire: Questions of Balance*

We'd like you to take some time to complete the following questionnaire. Most of these questions do not lend themselves to quick responses, so try to make your answers as complete as possible. We hope this exercise will help illuminate those issues that are most essential in achieving success and balance in the kind of workstyle and lifestyle you design for yourself.

1. How do you define success?

2. Name three people you consider successful, and write down what it is about them that you admire.

3. To what extent is your definition of success based on the following?

   - Money
   - Power
   - A prestigious career

4. If you did not have to earn money, how would you spend most of your time?

5. To what extent is your concept of success shaped by what you perceive to be the expectations of others?

6. Do you feel that your dedication to work is negatively impacting other aspects of your life?

7. Do you frequently wish that you had more time to spend with family and/or friends?

8. Do you often feel "stressed out" or exhausted at the end of a workweek?

9. Do you feel that there will never be enough time for you to do the things you've always dreamed about?

10. If you could balance your life any way you wish, how much of your time would you spend on the following?

- Work
- Family
- Travel
- Leisure
- Creative pursuits
- Self-improvement
- Spiritual enrichment

Keep in mind that balancing the various dimensions of your life is an ongoing process. At times it may be difficult to achieve a truly harmonious state. But you can do it once you've defined your priorities and learned to maintain a sense of proportion in whatever you do.

One of the great things about being a career temp is that it lets you structure a workstyle that supports an integrated, harmonious lifestyle. If you need to work on a steady basis, you can do that. If something comes up and you need to take a few weeks or even months off, the career temp workstyle can easily accommodate that as well.

Perhaps you want to travel or spend time in creative pursuits, but you are forced to work a prohibitive number of hours in order to support your existing lifestyle. In that case, you might consider making some adjustments in the way you live and work.

Look around and you'll see lots of people who are obsessed with consumption for its own sake. On the surface, these men and women may have material things that you covet. But a closer look often reveals that this obsession has thrown other aspects of their lives out of balance.

We know of many career temps who've achieved a harmonious lifestyle that includes healthy balance between career and financial objectives, family and psychic needs, as well as leisure and creative activities. Let's explore some cases in point.

Nancy, who lives in Wilkes-Barre, Pennsylvania, has been temping for five years. A skilled bookkeeper and word processor, Nancy sought a work situation that would allow her to spend time with her two school-age children and pursue a variety of interests.

"I'm quite active in my church and local school district, as well as in my daughter's Girl Scout troop," Nancy remarks. "I need to work in order to supplement my husband's income, but it's essential that I have an adaptable situation."

Nancy's husband, Jack, is a self-employed construction contractor who has busy and idle periods. When he works, Nancy is able to be there for her children. When her husband is not working, Nancy calls her personnel coordinator and asks to be sent out on assignments. During those times, her husband takes care of the kids. Recently, Nancy started going for her associates degree at a local community college.

"I realize that I'm juggling a lot of balls in my life," Nancy admits. "Still, there are a number of goals I want to accomplish, both as an individual and as a mother and wife. Temping is a career that lets me maintain the delicate balance I need to be effective at whatever I do."

Bill, who works out of the same Wilkes-Barre office as Nancy, had been employed by the state for over 35 years. In 1984, at age 60, Bill agreed to take early retirement. After six months, Bill—who was unmarried—felt isolated and lacking in structure.

"I was getting tired of hanging around the house," Bill recalls. "I found that I really missed the social aspect of going to work. Also, it felt strange to get up in the morning and not have a place to go."

An ad in a local newspaper convinced Bill to find out more about the temp workstyle option. Shortly thereafter, he applied and soon began working three days a week on various assignments.

Since 1986, Bill has been working as a courier for a local bank. In addition to supplementing his income, Bill enjoys the stress-free work and feels he is spending meaningful time with people.

Paul is a software engineer who lives in Portland, Oregon. "I can always count on temporary work to bring in additional income when my consulting business slows down," he says. "Also, temping lets me turn down contracts that I would otherwise be forced to accept."

Recently, Paul wanted to take six months off to travel to Asia. When he returned, his personnel coordinator was able to assign him immediately to a six-week project. While he was on that job, Paul was offered a lucrative consulting project that was slated to begin a week after his current assignment was due to end. Once that project was completed, Paul accepted another temporary assignment, after which he took a three-week vacation.

"I guess you can count me among the ranks of career temporaries. The cyclical nature of my business is such that I am always going to have to rely on temporary work to bring in additional income. At the same time, I feel lucky to have the opportunity to take time off for travel whenever I want."

Lucy is employed by the Corpus Christi, Texas, independent school district as an interpreter for the hearing impaired. During the summer and holiday breaks, Lucy—who types 65 words a minute and is proficient in several word processing packages—temps as a secretary. Because of her excellent skills and positive attitude, Lucy's service is able to keep her busy whenever she wants or needs to work.

"I consider myself a career temp," Lucy says proudly. "Secretarial assignments provide a good contrast with the work I do with hearing-impaired children.

"There are times when I prefer being with my husband and children—or just relaxing. However, there are other times when I need to earn extra money. It's great to be with a service that lets me achieve that delicate balance between family, leisure and work. "Frankly, I can't foresee a time when I would completely stop temping. I expect to be doing this indefinitely."

▌ *The Choice Is Yours!*

As you can see, there are any number of ways to be a successful career temp. This is one of the few workstyles that you can design and redesign to fit your changing needs. Naturally, the career temp option is not for everyone.

There are still many people who want permanent positions. As we will discuss in Chapter Eight, temping is proving to be one of the best ways of achieving that goal. But, as we noted earlier, the person who is aiming for a permanent job has different objectives and a different mind-set than the career temp.

Perhaps you're wondering if there's a downside to career temping. As with everything else in life, there is a pain and gain factor in every choice one makes. Some people are concerned about pensions, profit sharing and comprehensive medical benefits. Others are interested in finding mentors or attaining upward mobility within a particular company. If these issues are important to you, we suggest pursuing the kind of paths to permanent employment we will explore in the next chapter.

At this point, we feel that it is only fair to mention a pitfall to which some people—albeit a small percentage—succumb. We have met some men and women who are not well suited to career temping but who can't seem to address their career goals adequately. Unable to make a commitment to a long-term career, these individuals use the temporary solution as a permanent solution.

Perhaps you know of someone who is a "professional student." That person, after receiving his bachelor's degree, can't bring himself to face the angst of job hunting. Consequently, he goes for a master's degree. Upon receiving it, however, he finds that he is still unable to decide what he wants to do. There seems to be no alternative but to pursue his Ph.D., but that, too, proves not to be the solution. What will our professional student do at that point? Well, there's always law school, then medical school, and so on.

There are, of course, people whose careers do require many years of schooling, just as there are those whose long-range needs are best addressed by career temping. Nevertheless, we want to caution you not to use the fact that you have money coming in to obscure your objectives or cause you to postpone making a commitment indefinitely. If, however, you do think that career temping may be a productive option for you, the following are the advantages that should be considered:

1. Your lifestyle and workstyle choices will be virtually unlimited.
2. You will be able to accommodate changes in the way you want to balance your life.
3. You will have many opportunities to learn new skills.
4. You will be challenged and stimulated by new work environments.
5. You will constantly be meeting new people.
6. You will be relatively free from stress and corporate politics.

Again, we recognize that career temping is not the most appropriate workstyle for everyone. Still, even if you don't envision career temping as a viable choice at the present time, it's one of the very few career options that will always be open to you.

▋ Notes

1. *The Temporary Help Industry: An Annual Update,* 1991 NATS Survey.
2. *USA Today,* May 10, 1991, as cited in: Patricia Aburdene and John Naisbitt, *Megatrends for Women,* (New York: Villard Books, 1992).
3. *U.S. News & World Report,* June 17, 1991.
4. *Wall Street Journal,* April 30, 1991.
5. Robert Bly, *Iron John: A Book About Men,* (Redding, MA: Addison-Wesley Books, 1990).

6. Aburdene and Naisbitt.
7. Carolyn Corbin, *Strategies 2000*, (Austin, TX: Eakin Press, 1991, revised edition).
8. Aburdene and Naisbitt.
9. The "time artist" concept is adapted, in part, from: Namanworth, Phillip and Busnar, Gene. *Working for Yourself: A Guide to Success For People Who Work Outside The 9-to-5 World*, (New York: McGraw-Hill Books, 1984).
10. *Newsweek* (special edition), Winter/Spring 1990.
11. Carolyn Corbin, *The Lifeskills Lecture Series*, (Dallas, TX: Carolyn Corbin, Inc. 1992).

8

Temping as a Pathway to a Permanent Position

Getting your foot in the door has never been easy when you're trying to land that first job. But today it's probably tougher than ever.

"College Seniors Face Worst Job Market in Decades," a recent front page article in *The New York Times* (May 12, 1992) proclaimed. The article cited a study conducted by the Collegiate Employment Research Institute at Michigan State that revealed the following.

- Some 1.1 million young men and women graduated college in 1992—the largest graduating class in American history.

159

- Approximately 45 percent of those graduates had no definite job prospects.

"College graduates are facing the toughest job market in half a century," observed Samuel M. Erenhalt, regional director of the Bureau of Labor Statistics in New York City in the same *New York Times* article. "What makes the job search more difficult for [these graduates] is that [they] are competing with 933,000 unemployed managers and professionals, whose jobless rate has increased by 60 percent."

If you're a recent college graduate trying to find that first job or someone trying to reenter the workplace after a long absence, this news can't be very encouraging. Still, there's no reason to despair.

Did you know that the major temporary services place thousands of people in permanent, career-track positions during both good and bad economic times? In fact, 54 percent of temporaries are eventually hired permanently at companies to which they are assigned.[1]

On the surface, it may seem ironic that temping has emerged as one of the best ways to secure a permanent job. But, if you think about it, nothing can be more logical.

▮ *Wearing the Employer's Hat*

We'd like you to try a little role-playing exercise. Imagine, for a moment, that you are an employer seeking qualified people for your company.

Let's assume that you run some classified ads in an effort to solicit candidates. Chances are you will be barraged with resumés that will be screened, either by you or someone on your payroll. Then, a number of prospects will be called in for interviews. Each interview might last anywhere from a few minutes to several hours. In some cases, tests and skill evaluations might be administered, either in house or by an outside firm.

After most of the first group of prospects are eliminated, two or three remaining candidates will be called in for second interviews. At that point, someone will be selected for the position. He or she will then be put on the payroll, trained to perform the appropriate functions and introduced to the corporate culture.

By this time, you—the employer—have invested a good deal of time and money in soliciting, screening, processing and training this new employee. After all that, what guarantees do you have with respect to any or all of the following issues:

- Will this person be able to get the job done?
- Will he/she function well as part of the team?
- Will he/she be reliable?

Unfortunately, you are not going to be in a position to answer any of these questions—not for a while, anyway. Most employers hire new people without any real way of knowing if they will be effective on the job. A person's resumé may look great, but this is no assurance that he or she will render superior or even competent job performance.

With all the emphasis placed on job interviews, these are often not reliable indicators of how well a person will fit in with a given company. There are some manipulative people who will do and say virtually anything to land a job. Others get nervous during interviews and never seem to present themselves in the best light.

Any experienced employer will tell you that people who are affable and responsive during interviews sometimes turn out to be impossible to deal with once they are hired. Conversely, a shy individual may seem closed and uncooperative when, in fact, he or she really is the best suited candidate for the job.

We'd like you to continue wearing the hat of an employer who is looking for qualified people. Only this time, instead of using the costly and risky hiring methods described above, we want you to envision what it would be like if you worked with a temporary service to address your personnel needs.

Your first step will be to call up the service and explain your requirements. At that point, you and your staff can concern yourself with other important matters while the service solicits and screens people for you.

If you make it known that your company is looking to fill a permanent position, the service will send people who have expressed a desire for this kind of placement. Should you be dissatisfied with a particular employee, the service will replace him immediately. In most cases, you will not be obliged to pay for that person's time.

Once you find someone who seems right, you can take as much time as you need to make your decision. When you are ready to hire that person on a permanent basis, the service will work with you in transitioning that employee from temporary to permanent status. By then you will be dealing with a known commodity—someone whose performance and attitude have been proven over a period of weeks or months. Consequently, there will be little downside risk in adding that person to your permanent staff.

▌ *Overcoming the Experience Boomerang*

Now that you've seen why a growing number of employers are using temporary services to address their permanent personnel needs, let's look at why this may also be the best way for you to get your foot in the door.

It's important to recognize the kind of obstacles people trying to enter the job market are likely to encounter, particularly during tough economic times. Once you know what you're up against, you'll be better able to deal with the rigors of job hunting. Consider the case of Cliff, a recent college grad who sought a position as an advertising copywriter.

"I called up the vice president in charge of personnel at a large advertising company," Cliff recalls. "Since she was a friend of my cousin, I hoped I would have an inside track. At the very least, I expected to be given a fair shot. When I called, she was extremely polite, and indicated that her company was hiring junior people.

'I'll look over your portfolio and call you back in a few days,' she said. That sounded promising.

"Like most college students, I had never worked on a real ad. My portfolio consisted of hypothetical campaigns that were done as class assignments. Still, I felt they were a good representation of what I could do.

"About a week later my portfolio was returned to me along with a form letter that read:

Dear Sir:

Thanks for your interest in our company. Unfortunately, at this time, we are not hiring any junior copywriters . . .

"The letter was signed by an assistant. What's worse, I got the distinct impression that my portfolio had never even been opened. I felt rejected and angry, but I decided to call my contact's assistant, a woman named Angela.

"I was hoping to get some feedback from you about my work," I said.

"Angela said she was very sorry, but her department wasn't hiring people with no commercial experience.

"I had to work to keep my temper in check, but I was too frustrated to let a remark like that pass.

"I just graduated college," I said. "How am I ever supposed to get experience if someone like you won't even consider giving me an opportunity?"

"Angela repeated that she was very sorry. She told me I could call again after I sold some of my work. Then she hung up."

The kind of quandary Cliff was facing is the kind of

Catch-22 situation many college graduates run into. They need experience to land a job. At the same time, they require a job in order to obtain the necessary experience.

One of the most satisfying aspects of what we do is helping young people like Cliff overcome this hurdle. If you're someone who is seeking an opportunity to demonstrate what you can do, temping is one of the best ways to showcase your talents.

Once you're on the job, it's up to you to prove your value to the company. If you succeed in doing that, most employers will want to keep you on. In many cases, companies don't hire temps with the specific intention of retaining them permanently. Still, if a job opens up and you happen to be at the right place, all sorts of exciting things can happen.

Roger is currently the vice president of the song publishing arm of a major record company. Eight years ago, when he first came to the company, Roger was filling in for a clerical worker who was out sick.

"I had been working as a musician for a number of years," Roger recalls, "and I found myself between bands with no money coming in."

Since he had some typing and clerical skills, Roger decided that temping might be a good stopgap measure. On his application Roger noted that he preferred working at a record company, or in something related to music.

Roger made a good first impression on Sandra, his personnel coordinator at the temp service. Two days after she interviewed Roger, an opening from a record company came in.

"Even though I'd just met Roger," Sandra remembers, "I liked his attitude and his overall presentation. When the record company assignment crossed my desk, I called Roger immediately, and he started working the very next day."

Roger recognized that this was a unique opportunity. "The day I got to the record company, I told my supervisor that I was going to do a better job than any temp they'd ever had.

"At first it was kind of tough. In spite of what I told my supervisor, I really didn't want to spend my life doing clerical work. Still, I knew that chances like this don't come along every day. That's why I vowed to give a 100 percent effort to every task I was assigned and to take a positive approach to the whole situation. I guess they liked my work because I was eventually offered a permanent job—which I enthusiastically accepted.

"I was still primarily doing clerical work, but now I was assisting one of the most respected and powerful people in the song publishing department. As we got better acquainted, he realized that I had a good ear for hit songs. Eventually, I was given the responsibility of screening tapes. After a number of promotions, I worked my way up to my current position—a vice president in the song-publishing department."

Some of you may feel that success stories like Roger's are unusual, but in fact they are far more common than you might think. Most highly successful people were not born with silver spoons in their mouths, nor were they the recipients of random strokes of luck. Roger is an example of someone whose success debunks two common myths about what is commonly referred to as *good luck.*

MYTH #1: BEING AT THE RIGHT PLACE AT THE RIGHT TIME IS STRICTLY A MATTER OF COINCIDENCE

If you buy a lottery ticket that gets picked for a seven-figure prize, you can, indeed, attribute that to the good fortune of timing. But such an explanation completely misses the role timing played in Roger's success.

Certainly, it was lucky for Roger that he happened to apply to the temp service just before a record company assignment came in. Still, Roger must be credited with creating a good impression on Sandra, his personnel coordinator, and making her aware of his preferences.

"If Roger had not received this particular assignment, I think he would have waited until another record company position came along before attempting to secure a permanent position," Sandra says in retrospect. "In any case, he struck me as the type of person who would be reliable and try his best, even if he wasn't crazy about the assignment. When someone walks in here with that kind of an attitude, it always makes me want to help him succeed."

Myth #2: It's Not what You Know, but Who You Know

In school we are taught that life is supposed to be fair, but the lessons we learn in the real world are very different. Let's face it: There are plenty of examples of nepotism and cronyism in the business world. There may well be times when you are passed over in favor of someone who has better connections, but don't make the mistake of using that as an excuse for not pursuing your goals.

Getting back to our friend Roger, you'll recall that he walked into the record company not knowing a soul. Still, when he told his supervisor that he was going to do a better job than any temp they'd ever had, you can bet that he made an ally right there and then.

Without establishing this kind of groundwork, it's questionable whether Roger would have ever received an opportunity to display his considerable talents. As it was, Roger's boss in the publishing department wanted to give him an opportunity to showcase his abilities because he took a personal liking to him.

In retrospect you can see that Roger created his own luck from the start. Even when he was not crazy about his tasks, Roger always made it a point to do superior work and maintain a positive attitude. At every plateau he was forming new alliances and motivating people to be on his side.

Whatever your field and whatever your goals, the same opportunities to create your own luck are available to you. We urge you to recognize and take full advantage of them.

Designing Your Own Temp-to-Regular Job Search

We think that temping is a great way for people to conduct a job search and, ultimately, to land the job that's right for them. At Uniforce, we have developed a *"Smart-hire"* program to address this need. There are four unique advantages taking a temporary road to a permanent position provides. Let's look at each of these advantages, and see how it can work for you. The temp-to-perm option gives you:

1. Exposure to a variety of companies
2. An opportunity to build your resumé
3. Hands-on experience
4. The chance to find the unique career track that's right for you

 Job Hunting from the Inside In

Earlier in this chapter we discussed why employers don't really know what they're getting until an employee's performance can be observed on a day-to-day basis. Similarly, there is no way for you to gauge what working for a particular company will be like until you've had some first-hand experience there.

Several years ago, Jim was hired as a technical writer by a large electronics conglomerate immediately after graduating from college.

"I thought this was the opportunity of a lifetime," Jim remembers. "In terms of starting salary and benefits, you couldn't hope for a better entry-level job. Aside from that, I had a great rapport with the people who interviewed me.

"There's a saying that's often applied to people: 'You

can't judge a book by its cover.' I found out the hard way that the same principle applies to choosing a company.

"From day one I never felt comfortable with my co-workers or with the general atmosphere at this company. There seemed to be a lot of backbiting politics going on. I soon found out that the person I had replaced had been fired in some kind of power play coup. Apparently that individual was extremely popular. Even though I had nothing to do with his dismissal, people seemed to hold it against me.

"At departmental meetings, my ideas and opinions were totally ignored. I soon found myself with nothing to do. Sure I was collecting a nice paycheck, but I began to feel like a prisoner in my small office. At one point, I started having digestive problems, and I knew that I would eventually develop an ulcer if I didn't quit this job.

"It took me a while to make the move—probably longer than it should have. Why was I hesitant? Aside from the money, I thought it would look bad on my resumé to leave a job only a few months after I was hired. But eventually I gave notice that I was leaving, which my bosses were only too glad to accept."

After he left this uncomfortable corporate environment, Jim began working for a temporary service. It took him two and a half years, but he was finally offered a permanent position at a company that he knew was right for him.

"It was never my intention to temp for very long," Jim recalls. "Still, the last thing I wanted to do was wind up in another nightmare situation.

"When I started working for my service, I made it clear that I was looking for a permanent position. My personnel coordinator promised to do all she could to help me reach my objectives and explained what she expected of me in terms of making the transition.

"I had two offers within my first eight months of temping. Both were at companies at which I was relatively comfortable. But I had made up my mind that I was going to wait until I felt really excited about an offer. In the meantime, I started to enjoy temping. I got to meet a lot of interesting people and to see what different companies were like. At one point, I was even thinking about becoming a career temporary.

"Two years of temping had flown by, and I was feeling good about my work situation. Then my personnel coordinator called with what started out to be a three-month assignment. Before I knew it, three months had turned into six months.

"By the time I was asked to stay on permanently, I had already decided that this was where I wanted to work. Naturally, I immediately told my service about the offer and let them work out the terms of my transition."

Whenever we hear stories like Jim's, it only increases our desire to help people avoid the kind of problems he encountered. Many job-hunting books recommend that you research and approach the specific companies you wish to work for. Temping carries this targeting principle one step further by actually providing you with opportunities to take a firsthand look at a variety of work environments.

Make sure your service knows from the start that you are looking for a permanent position. In most cases it will try to place you on assignments that have temp-to-perm potential. If you have set your sights on a career in a particular industry, share these objectives with your personnel coordinator. Most temporary-service professionals will do their best to work with you.

People who conduct targeted job searches may also have specific companies in mind. If you're aware that a service works with a particular corporate client, there is nothing wrong with requesting that you be placed there. If, however, you ask a service whether a specific company is a client of theirs, an answer may not be immediately forthcoming.

In general, temporary services do not have a particularly adversarial relationship with one another. As in most other businesses, however, services do compete with each other for clients. Consequently, there are times when one service's loss is another's gain.

It is not unknown for one temporary service to send a "shopper" to another service in order to secure a competitive advantage. That's why you should not be surprised if a personnel coordinator wants to get to know you before sharing potentially valuable information about a service's corporate clients.

Since you are free to work with a number of services, it shouldn't take you long to figure out which one will be best able to place you at the companies you wish to target. All the while, you'll be availing yourself of opportunities to try before you buy. And, as we noted earlier, this feeling-out process is a two-way street.

Just as temping gives you a chance to sample a variety of companies before making a long-term commitment, the companies have an opportunity to see if you are the kind of person they would like to bring aboard on a permanent basis.

▌ *Building a Track Record of Success*

Let's assume that you've decided to temp your way to a permanent career. It's impossible to know, walking in, whether your first assignment will lead to a long-term position. Perhaps it will be your second, third—or even your tenth—assignment that puts you on the right career track. Since temping gives you an opportunity to earn a regular income while you conduct your search, there's no need to rush things. Take your time and make sure that you select a company and position that are right for you.

You'll recall the story of Roger, the former musician assigned as a clerical temp to a record company who eventually worked his way up to vice president. When he first registered with the temporary service, Roger was more interested in paying the rent than in securing a permanent career. He quickly recognized, however, that being placed in a record company presented a rare opportunity to catapult himself to a position he hadn't originally envisioned.

Roger arrived at the record company totally lacking in the kind of background one usually needs to rise to the executive level. Nevertheless, he succeeded in using this opportunity as a proving ground for his talents. From his position as a clerical temp, he started building the kind of impressive track record that underlies success in any business.

Remember the story of Jim, the technical writer who accepted a high-paying job that turned out to be a nightmare? By the time he started temping, Jim recognized how essential it is to test the waters at different companies before signing on for the long haul. Jim's personnel coordinator also felt that it was important for Jim to build his resumé with a series of positive work experiences.

Jim did an outstanding job at each company for which he temped and was able to obtain impressive recommendations from his supervisors. As it turned out, the company that eventually hired Jim specifically asked about his previous job experience.

Had Jim not been able to show some relevant work history on his resumé, it is doubtful that he would have been accepted for this particular assignment. You'll recall that, before he started temping, Jim did have a permanent job. However, that experience was so negative that Jim decided not to include it on his resumé.

"I built an impressive work history exclusively from my temporary assignments," Jim remarks. "If not for that, I might still be out there looking for a permanent position."

If you feel that you have special talents, but lack the requisite background, temping can help you close that gap. Just let your personnel coordinator know what you want to do and where you'd like to do it. The chances are good that she can help you. Even if she is unable to place you in the exact assignment you're looking for, she can probably assign you to a company where you'll have an opportunity to demonstrate your skills.

Again we want to urge you to approach the temp-to-perm process with a degree of patience. While we feel that it is one of the surest and fastest routes to career success, it's unrealistic to expect that you will attain your goals overnight. It may take several assignments for a number of services before you finally hit your target, but it will happen if you persevere and exercise patience.

We also want to encourage you to keep all options open in your job-related dealings. Since temporary services don't ask you to sign an employment contract, you can sever relations with them at any time. Nevertheless, it is good practice to complete all assignments you have accepted—even if you don't find them desirable or feel that they won't be especially helpful in achieving your long-term career objectives.

Every business is a small community unto itself. That's true of the temporary services industry as well as any field in which you might want to build a career. Word of mouth is important, and it's in your interest that any and all words said about you are positive. There's simply no point in burning your bridges or having time periods on your resumé that can't be accounted for.

Make sure you receive favorable reviews on every assignment to which you are sent. This is perhaps the most basic rule when you are trying to create a good reputation and track record. You want to be able to list the temporary services for which you work, as well as the clients to whom you are assigned as references that establish a stable and productive work history. In fact, temp services are among those companies that sometimes hire temporaries for permanent positions.

When Erin graduated college with a degree in personnel management, she found it impossible to find a job in her field. Needing money to live and to pay off student loans, she accepted a sales position with an insurance company. "I wish I could put it in nicer terms," says Erin, "but I simply hated that job."

When Erin registered with her temporary service, she specified that she wanted positions that had temp-to-perm potential. As it happened, there was an immediate position available for a receptionist. That turned out to be Erin's first placement.

"I felt that I was overqualified to be a receptionist," Erin recalls, "but I needed the money, so I accepted the assignment."

Erin's supervisors at the service liked her attitude and recognized her potential. Six weeks later they offered to train her as a backup interviewer. Within ten months Erin was offered a permanent position as a personnel coordinator for the service. Today she is one of the top people at her job.

 ## *Learning Things You Were Never Taught in School*

We've discussed the experience boomerang that many college graduates run into—particularly in the face of a tough economy. These young people lack the experience many employers consider a prerequisite for hiring. Unfortunately, it's next to impossible to obtain that experience unless someone is willing to give you that first job.

Temporary service professionals are committed to helping highly motivated young people get the chance to show what they can do. While we feel for those individuals who have problems entering the job market because they lack experience, we also understand why some employers always specify—experience required!

We are great believers in the value of formal education. However, we are also aware of the limitations of book learning. There is a tremendous difference between getting straight A's in school and succeeding in the business world. In fact, many of the world's most successful men and women were not particularly good students.

Why, you may ask, is this so? For one thing, the criteria for success in the academic world are completely different from those in the workplace.

In school, you may be asked to write a paper analyzing a problem. Your professor reads the paper and concludes that your analysis was only partially correct. It is clear, however, that you read all your assignments and made an honest effort. More often than not, such a performance will be rewarded with a grade of C or B.

If, on the other hand, you are asked to analyze a problem in the business world, there are no in-between grades. You either come up with a solution that works—or you don't.

Let's face it: The quality of your performance in school has no real impact. After all, what's at stake if you do a job that is good, bad or mediocre? A grade!

In the real world, however, doing the job right can make a great deal of difference. If you are a copywriter who creates a mediocre advertisement, for example, there is no C or B grade. Your company simply does not land an assignment and, consequently, loses a great deal of money.

Although they may not express it in so many words, this fundamental difference between the business and academic environments is what makes employers hesitant to hire people who lack on-the-job experience.

Temporary services give their corporate clients an opportunity to "try before they buy." If a young person shows he can cut the mustard, there is a reasonably good chance that he will be offered a permanent position. If not, the corporate client has not assumed much downside risk.

There is another reason why hands-on experience is regarded as being so important. A growing number of today's jobs require a knowledge of up-to-date technologies. Unfortunately, many schools are not doing their part to help their students address this need.

A magazine writer we know was looking for someone to help her with some word processing. She thought about finding a local high school student who was taking secretarial courses. It seemed logical to this writer that teachers would understand the value of their students' receiving some real work experience.

When the writer approached the middle-aged typing teacher at the local high school, she received the following response:

"I'll ask around for you but to tell you the truth, I just teach typing. Oh, sure, we have some word processors and computers, but I don't know how to use them."

At that point the teacher signaled that he wanted to whisper something: "Between you and me," he confided, "I actually know more about word processing than I let on. But, if I make that known, they'd try to get me to teach it, and I'd rather not go to the trouble of learning all those new programs and techniques."

Unfortunately, regressive attitudes of this kind are far too common throughout our educational system—and the results are being felt in the workplace. Incidentally, the magazine writer never did receive a call from a high school student interested in part-time work.

Is our educational system doing its job in terms of teaching students the attitudes and skills they need to succeed in the workplace? Apparently not. According to the Bureau of Labor Statistics, most people entering the work force require at least some preparation before they are ready to work. In fact, the following observations, which were made by economist Pat Choate in 1986, are even more applicable today:

"The U.S. spends [billions of dollars] annually to operate an elaborate system of education and training programs—which includes [thousands of] vocational schools, technical institutes and community colleges. These facilities and their personnel represent a major economic asset—a basic means to help workers prepare for a first job and retool their skills throughout their careers.

"Unfortunately, this system lacks the flexibility and capacity to provide up-to-date education and training. Institutions that must rely on antiquated equipment and out-dated faculty skills inevitably provide training that is already obsolete."[2]

As the crisis in our educational system worsens, temporary services are becoming more instrumental in helping entry-level people learn the technical and other skills they need to succeed in the world of business. But, because our world continues to change so rapidly, the demands of today's workplace are likely to become outdated almost as quickly as they are able to be addressed. This brings us to a question that should not be overlooked: How permanent is a permanent job?

Carolyn Corbin is among those futurists who predict that most people will change occupations and jobs several times during their working years. Her research indicates that a person's career position will change in responsibility and technology approximately every five years.

"In the past, people could expect to go to work in their twenties and continue working until age 65 without having to acquire any new skills. Now all this has changed. Some jobs will be restructured every six months—especially those that are technology related."[3]

The better services are committed to helping their people obtain the training opportunities they will need to keep working, whether on a temporary or permanent basis.

▌ *Finding Your Unique Career Track*

There are a variety of reasons why people seek permanent jobs. Some women and men know early on that they want to pursue a certain career. Consequently, they feel it's important to get on that track as soon as possible. We meet many other young people who want the security of a permanent job but still have not defined their ultimate career goals.

If you're not sure about the kind of work you would like to do on a long-term basis or the kind of work environment in which you will feel most comfortable, temping may be the best way to resolve those questions.

As a temporary, you will be able to work in both small and large offices, private corporations, government agencies and nonprofit organizations. In the course of sampling and reflecting upon those experiences, you are bound to find the workstyle and career track for which you are best suited.

We've come across a number of recent graduates who think they have their career goals formulated. In reality, many of them don't have the slightest idea of what their supposed dream job is going to be like.

For example, there are people whose love of music drives them to seek a career in the record industry. As it happens, we are often able to provide such assignments. Nevertheless, the day-to-day realities of working in this and other so-called glamour industries often have little to do with the creation or enjoyment of music or any other art form.

Oftentimes, it takes a good deal of work experience before a person really has a sense of where he or she wants to go. Futurist Carolyn Corbin believes that, in order to develop this sense of direction, a person needs to acquire the tracking lifeskill.

"In order to achieve your full career potential," says Corbin, "you must first do three things:

1. Realistically assess your abilities, desires and talents.

2. Determine what it is that makes you stand out.

3. Pursue a career that enables you to maximize those strengths."[4]

These tracking skills take time to develop. While there are some notable exceptions, few young men and women come out of school with a real basis for addressing these issues. Temping gives you an opportunity to get a firm grounding in the business world while you develop the wisdom and life skills to select the career track that's right for you.

It's important to remember that there is no set timetable for selecting a long-term career track. Some people achieve that objective in their twenties. A growing number of people are still searching in their thirties and forties. However long it takes, it's reassuring to know that temporary services are there to enable you to take as much time as you need to make the right decision.

▋ *Temp-to-Perm Protocol*

If you know walking in that your primary purpose in temping is to secure a permanent position, we strongly recommend that you inform your personnel coordinator immediately. In most cases she will discuss your objectives with you and outline some ways that you can work together to achieve them.

Some of you may start temping without having a particular objective in mind. In Chapter Seven, we met some people who thought they wanted permanent positions, only to find that their workstyle and lifestyle needs were best served by career temping.

Conversely, there are those individuals who are not looking for a permanent position when they start temping. It is, however, not uncommon for a temporary assignment to evolve into a permanent job offer. If you prove your value to a company, it makes good business sense that they are going to want to keep you around.

Whether or not you started out with the intention of securing a permanent job, you have an obligation to call your service if a client presents you with such an offer. If you wish to decline the position, the service can take steps to secure it for another of their qualified employees. If, on the other hand, you intend to accept the job, you must give your service the opportunity to make the appropriate arrangements with the client company.

In general, the service and its corporate client will come

to an agreement as to the best and most equitable way to transition an employee from the temp service's payroll to the permanent employer's payroll. In most cases, the hiring company will pay the temporary service a lump-sum conversion charge or agree to keep the person on the temporary service's payroll for a period of time, usually 90 days. The exact terms of each conversion will depend primarily on a given employee's skill level.

As noted in Chapter Five, it is unethical—and illegal—for a client company to shift temps from the service's payroll directly to the company's own payroll without first notifying the temp service.

Since the temporary employment service recruited, screened, placed you and, in some cases, helped upgrade your skills, they are entitled to be compensated by a client company that wants to hire you as a permanent employee. Keep in mind, too, that if you accept the position, the temp service will not be earning anything on you in the future.

We believe that the relationship between a temporary service, its client companies and its employees should be one of mutual benefit. We get a good deal of satisfaction helping people find the right career track. At the same time, it is gratifying to be able to fulfill our clients' needs for productive, reliable people.

Part of having a win-win relationship involves recognizing and respecting the other party's needs. You, the temporary employee, may be seeking a career-track position that gives you a good income and self-satisfaction. The company that hires you wants to find the best people available without devoting an undue amount of money and time to that process. The temporary service is in a pivotal position to satisfy your objectives, as well as those of its corporate clients.

Keep in mind that temporary services are in business to make a profit. Like all companies, we would not exist if we did not satisfy the needs of our employees and clients. By the same token, we expect the people and companies with whom we work to respect our position.

As a temporary employee, you assume an implicit commitment to let your service know if a client offers to hire you on a permanent basis. As an ethical person—and someone who wants to establish a good reputation in the business world—it behooves you to conduct yourself in accordance with the principles of common sense and mutual interest.

We believe that the saying "Do unto others as you would have them do unto you" is more than just a collection of empty words. For us, this concept is at the heart of how we try to run our business, as well as our lives. Until proven otherwise, we will continue to assume that those individuals and companies with whom we come in contact will abide by the same standards.

▮ Notes

1. NATS statistics cited in *Newsday*, Sunday, November 22, 1992.

2. Pat Choate and J. K. Linger, *High-Flex Society: Shaping America's Economic Future*, (New York: Alfred A. Knopf, 1986).

3. Carolyn Corbin, *Strategies 2000*, (Austin, TX: Eakin Press, 1991 revised edition).

4. Carolyn Corbin, *The Lifeskills Lecture Series*, (Dallas, TX: Carolyn Corbin, Inc., 1992).

9

Crisis and Transitional Temping: Money and Psychic Income when You Need It Most

"*M*any of us grew up valuing the path of least resistance. But, in fact, you are much more likely to get what you want if you are willing to travel the road of *most* resistance. Look closely, and you will find that there are few overnight success stories. Success in any aspect of life is almost always the result of well-directed effort—and an ability to use adversity as the impetus for positive change."[1]

In Chapters Seven and Eight, we explored the ways temporary services address the long-term needs of those who seek careers in temporary employment and in permanent positions. In this chapter we look at how temping helps people who, for a variety of reasons, find themselves under immediate pressure to secure a job. These men and women may face a wide range of situations that come about during hard economic times or as a result of unanticipated life occurrences. Such circumstances include:

- Sudden unemployment
- Divorce or abandonment by a spouse
- Recent arrival in a new city
- The immediate need to work or earn additional money

Any of these situations may be viewed as a crisis, a state that is generally perceived to be negative. However, it may surprise you to learn that the first two dictionary definitions of the word *crisis* are:

1. A stage in a sequence of events at which the trend of all future events is determined.
2. A turning point.[2]

We're not trying to deny that crisis situations can cause a good deal of turmoil and pain. At the same time, we strongly believe that every crisis contains within it the seeds of empowerment and opportunity.

We can empathize with people in tenuous circumstances who find these words ethereal. Men and women who need to pay the rent and put food on the table want a job, not a philosophy lesson. As you will see, developing a positive approach to adversity can be just as important as addressing those immediate needs. In any case, helping people generate money to stay afloat is one of the things temporary services do best.

We can think of no solution for those who need a job quickly that offers the advantages of temping. Most services can place you in a matter of days and, in some cases, on the very same day that you apply. The exact time frame will, of course, depend on the inventory of assignments the service has on hand, as well as your skill level, work history and salary requirements. In most cases, though, temping will prove to be the most effective way to address your needs in three critical areas:

1. *Financial:* People who find themselves under severe monetary pressure can generate immediate income that enables them to pay for necessities.

2. *Psychological:* Getting back into the work force helps a person feel useful and needed. This boost in self-esteem is often as significant as the money a temporary job brings in.

3. *Social:* People who find themselves unemployed, abandoned, suddenly strapped for cash or relocated in a strange city tend to feel isolated. Having a job provides an outlet for developing new business and social contacts.

The process of becoming affiliated and working with a temporary service was fully explored in Chapter Four. Generally speaking, the initial procedures are pretty much the same regardless of your immediate situation. There are, however, differences in how a service goes about helping various employees meet their needs.

Experienced personnel coordinators understand that career temps and those seeking permanent job opportunities often have the same requirements as people in transition or crisis. By definition, crisis situations—be they economic, emotional or social in nature—require quick action. Temporary employment services give people in such circumstances an opportunity to start picking up the pieces by providing immediate work.

We see temping as a highly effective way not only to deal with a crisis that has already befallen you but also to minimize those unforeseen crises that can potentially derail any of us at any time. Unanticipated changes are a fact of life, particularly in a fast-moving society like ours. When that happens, temporary service professionals can show you how to surmount obstacles that might otherwise be devastating.

In this chapter, you will see how women and men experiencing various forms of crises use temping to help them overcome these situations. And in the course of addressing their short-term needs, most of these individuals wind up experiencing a good deal of long-term growth.

What's that? You say that your immediate problems are so intense that you're hardly in a position to worry about anything else? We can certainly understand your feelings. Nevertheless, we respectfully submit that this is a short-sighted approach.

While we make our living in the temporary services industry, we are interested in helping you develop permanent—or at least long-term—solutions. This brings us back to the belief we expressed on page 184:

> ***Every crisis contains within it the seeds of empowerment and opportunity.***

Crisis management has become an important concept for both businesses and individuals who wish to survive and thrive in a world where uncertainty is perhaps the only real certainty. In his book, *The Winds of Turbulence,* Howard Putnam, former CEO of Braniff and Southwest Airlines, urges business people to "get ready for anything!" We believe the advice Putnam offers is equally relevant for women and men who are determined to weather any and all adversities that may befall them:

"We live in erratic times. We fly in turbulent . . . skies. In the past few years, we have seen more dramatic political and economic shifts in the world than have occurred in all the decades since World War II. Some of these shifts have already affected [us]; others will make themselves felt in the future—and nobody can predict with any certainty just how.

"As the world . . . continues to undulate relentlessly, success will depend on our ability to channel the raw energy of this turbulence in productive and profitable ways."[3]

When you come right down to it, a crisis can be perceived in one of two ways:

1. A catastrophe—a pain in the neck that you wish would disappear.
2. A chance to change and grow.

When we are hit with setbacks and crises, our entire belief system can be put to the test, in terms of our own self-esteem, as well as our ability to influence what happens to us. There are, unquestionably, many occurrences that are outside of our control. On the other hand, there is a great deal we can do to shape the way those events affect our lives.

In the final analysis, the way we label, interpret and react to crises will determine our ability to counter these potentially devastating experiences. This brings us to a question that is central to our discussion.

▐ *How Well Do You Handle Adversity?*

Actually this question is comprised of several closely related issues. We'd like you to take a few minutes to complete the following exercise. We think it will prove enlightening.

Please respond to each of the statements below as follows:

- Place the number *1* next to the statement if it describes your reaction most of the time.
- Place the number *2* next to each statement if it describes your reaction some of the time.
- Place the number *3* next to each statement if it describes your reaction none, or almost none, of the time.

▌ *Turning Negatives into Positives*

1. When bad things happen, I often think: Why me?
2. I usually feel my problems are of my own making rather than a matter of circumstance.
3. In times of crisis, I tend to mope and become withdrawn.
4. I don't like to grieve for my losses because I believe that will only prove how weak I really am.
5. I don't believe someone who says a tragedy in his life served to make him stronger.
6. I often find myself wondering why things seem to go so much more smoothly for others than they do for me.
7. I would classify myself as a pessimist rather than an optimist.
8. I see all pain and turmoil as bad and unnecessary.
9. If I got fired from my job, I would take it as a sure sign of my lack of worth.
10. When someone points out that I made a mistake, I tend to blame myself rather than view it as a learning opportunity.

Please add up your score and write down the total in the space provided below.

Total:___

Scoring Scale:

21–30 = Very positive and productive response to adversity.

11–20 = Moderately adaptive and productive response to adversity.

10–19 = Few long-term gains derived from crisis and adversity.

Please note that this exercise is designed to give you a general indication of the extent to which you currently use crisis and adversity as positive opportunities for growth and learning. Most people's responses are to a great extent based on their past experience. A person's score on this exercise should not be taken to be indicative of set personality traits.

Now that you've had an opportunity to examine the way you respond to adversity, we'd like to share with you some useful ideas about how temping can help you handle a number of crisis situations—both now and in the future.

▌ *Out of a Job*

Receiving a pink slip has always been a harrowing experience, but in recent years massive firing and layoffs have reached epidemic proportions. According to the Bureau of Labor Statistics, the jobless rate for managers and professionals increased by 60 percent between 1990 and 1992.[4] The statistics are equally grim in many white and blue-collar fields.

In his song, "My Hometown," singer-songwriter Bruce Springsteen noted that: "Those jobs are going, boys, and they ain't coming back."[5] Author/futurist Carolyn Corbin expanded on that same sentiment in her book *Strategies 2000* when she said:

"There is no guarantee of security anywhere today. Leadership changes, economic problems, mergers and acquisitions may cause a worker of several years' tenure to become unemployed. In the end, the employee must always look out for his own well-being. That has become a fact of corporate and government life in the new-age economy."[6]

Should you suddenly find yourself out of work, we strongly suggest that you register with one or more temporary services as soon as possible. We believe that temping is a practical option that no unemployed man or woman can afford to ignore.

When 30-year-old Jason was laid off from his bank job, he felt devastated. "Only two months earlier I had turned down a position with another bank," he recalls. "I thought that after seven years, I had earned some job security.

"Every day I heard about heavy layoffs at banks and other companies. With a wife, two kids and a mortgage, I figured that my best bet was to stay put. When the notice of my firing came, I was unprepared. I was told that I was one of the last people to be let go, as if that was supposed to make me feel better.

"My bank gave me 120 days' severance pay, so I thought I'd have time to replace my position. I must have sent 200 resumés out during the first 30 days. All that effort resulted in three interviews and zero job offers.

"Ninety days had passed, and I was really starting to worry. I was thinking about trying to find some carpentry work, since I had done that when I was younger. I recall that there was an ad in the local paper for an assistant carpenter. The pay was only seven dollars per hour, but over a hundred people responded to that ad the very first day.

"Finally my 120 days were almost up and I could feel myself getting desperate. We had a little bit of savings, but most of our money was tied up in our house. Aside from financial worries, I was feeling depressed and out of touch with people. I guess I blamed myself for my predicament. I knew that I had to do something soon, but I really had no idea where to turn.

"It was my wife who suggested that I look into temping. It seems that she was telling an acquaintance about my situation. Her husband had been laid off a year earlier and started temping as a stopgap measure. He wound up liking his new-found flexibility so much that he became a career temporary.

"I've got to tell you that I was extremely skeptical. I'd never known anyone who temped as a career. Frankly, I never even considered temping because I always thought it was just for secretaries. Still, I was out of options, and I figured that I was hardly in a position to dismiss any possibility. In any case, it had to be better than pumping gas at the local service station."

Jason made a favorable impression on his temporary service interviewer. As it happened, she had a number of assignments available for someone with his skills and work history. Two days after his initial interview, Jason was placed on a one-week assignment. He has been working on a regular basis ever since.

"I've been temping for the past six months," says Jason, "and I'm prepared to keep doing this as long as necessary. I don't see myself temping as a career. However, I am making lots of contacts and acquiring some new job skills. I believe that these assets will eventually help me secure another permanent position. My wife recently started temping on evenings and weekends to help supplement our income. Between the two of us, we should have no problem making ends meet."

We asked Jason what was the most important lesson he learned from this entire experience. Here's what he said:

"I think I became too dependent on my job—not only for a paycheck, but for benefits and a sense of belonging. I've come to understand that this kind of outlook is unrealistic, and even dangerous, given the realities that exist today. Now I know that no company can ensure my welfare or that of my family. Ultimately, that responsibility falls squarely on me and my wife.

"Temping has been an important factor in helping me take back control of my life. In addition to enabling me to generate a regular income during this difficult period, temping has helped me become more self-reliant. It would be a stretch to say that I'm glad I was fired. On the other hand, I've emerged from the experience a much stronger person— someone who is able to cope with unanticipated bumps in the road."

Author/futurist Carolyn Corbin finds that many people who are displaced from their jobs go through the kind of anguish that Jason experienced before he discovered the temporary workstyle:

"When people are fired or laid off, they generally list money as their number-one concern," observes Corbin. "Yet, in many instances, the loss of identity and self-esteem turn out to be even more devastating.

"Many people who work in the corporate world have come to depend on their careers for income as well as ego strength. When everything in your life—from your doctor bills to your friends—is provided by the workplace, the loss of this stabilizing force can make you feel as if you no longer have an identity.

"Each of us must learn to take charge of the psychic rewards that come from exchanging our skills for income. The first step in this process is understanding that no corporation can give us those things: We must learn to be independent and entrepreneurial in taking charge of our careers."[7]

We believe that the temporary workstyle provides a marvelous opportunity for people to develop these essential life skills. When you work on a per-assignment basis, it's almost impossible to become complacent or develop a false sense of security. In a world where people have become overly dependent on entitlements, such job attributes may be considered disadvantages. But, in a work environment that is becoming increasingly more performance based, these attitudes are undergoing some radical changes.

In the final analysis, the only real job security comes from knowing that you have marketable skills that people need. Temping can help you perfect these talents—while providing you with opportunities to develop the attitudes and lifeskills that underlie success in any endeavor.

 ## Out of a Marriage

Divorce is one of the most devastating emotional and financial experiences a person can face. Nevertheless, it is estimated that one out of two married couples in America will go that route at least once.[8]

Turn on the TV and you're bound to hear of a high profile divorce where a wife is collecting millions of dollars in maintenance and child support from her estranged celebrity husband. Unfortunately for most women, that's not the usual scenario.

In recent years, the legislatures in many states have sought to revise divorce laws in order to give greater weight to a woman's financial interest in a marriage. There have, for example, been a number of cases in which wives worked for years to put their husbands through medical or law school. At one point after these degrees were attained, the husbands sought a divorce.

The judges in some of those cases set a legal precedent by ruling that the wife's efforts were instrumental in establishing and enriching the husband's career. Therefore, when it came time to divide the marital assets, she was deemed to be a full partner in his future earnings—at least for a specified time period.

In spite of such positive changes in the law, women are still likely to get the short end of the financial stick in a divorce. Why, you may be wondering, are economic conditions still skewed against divorced women and their children? Attorney Bernard Rothman, author of *Loving & Leaving*, is among those experts who believe that part of the reason for this continuing inequity is a backlash from the women's movement.

"Many . . . male judges—particularly older ones—are offended by the whole notion of women's liberation," Rothman observes. "Therefore, they are prone, when awarding maintenance, to take the following attitude: 'If you want equal rights, that's fine. But you had better . . . be ready to assume the hardships and responsibilities that go along with those benefits.'

"Since the new laws were supposedly designed to help

women, this kind of posture on behalf of the court is ironic—and even tragic in the worst cases."[9]

Recent census bureau statistics reveal just how grim the picture is for many divorced women:[10]

- In 1990, there were almost 10 million single parents. This represents a 40 percent increase since 1980.
- About 85 percent of all single parents are single mothers.
- Single women head approximately 30 percent of households in the United States—one-third of which are poor.
- One out of every five children is living in poverty.

"It has been variously estimated that about half of all divorced fathers do not pay the full amount of support mandated by their divorce decree," attorney Rothman observes. "Furthermore, the level of court-ordered support has been totally inadequate for many custodial mothers to maintain an acceptable lifestyle . . .

"[At some point,] it was determined . . . that the average amount of support ordered nationwide did not cover even one-third of what it costs to clothe, feed, and maintain a child. In effect, the courts and deadbeat fathers were conspiring to create a burgeoning population of single-parent families headed by women who were forced to live on the edge of poverty—if not at the poverty level."[11]

What are women who find themselves in such dire straits to do? For a growing number of divorced and abandoned wives, the answer is temping.

When Gloria's husband left her and her two children, he simply disappeared without any prior notice. "Richard and I had our share of problems, but I never expected him to just walk out after ten years of marriage. The feelings of rejection were devastating, but I literally couldn't afford to get depressed.

"I had bills to pay and kids to support. That had to be

my first priority. We had some money in the bank, but I soon learned that he had taken most of it out of our joint checking account before skipping town.

"A friend of mine had gone through a similar experience. She got into a terrible rut trying to find her husband so she could get the maintenance and child support she felt she had coming. Eventually she started drinking and fell into a deep depression.

"I'm not the kind of person to let myself be wronged without doing anything about it, and I certainly hated Richard for walking out on us the way he did. Still, there was no way that I was going to let myself fall into the same trap as my friend. I was determined to pick up the pieces and move ahead in my life."

The Saturday after her husband left, Gloria attended a support group for divorced women. When she discussed her plight, several other women suggested that she look into temping. That Monday Gloria walked into the local office of a major service without an appointment. She proceeded to explain her situation to Joyce, the personnel coordinator whom Gloria now credits with being instrumental in helping her reclaim her life.

"I was 35 years old and had been out of the job market since Richard and I got married. I had a college degree in child social work, but I knew there were no jobs available in that field, and I had no experience doing anything else."

A skilled temporary-service professional, Joyce had helped many women in circumstances similar to Gloria's. "It was clear that Gloria had taken a real hit," Joyce recalls. "But I could see that she was the kind of person who would do anything necessary to become self-sufficient.

"I happened to have a short-term receptionist assignment available and Gloria grabbed it. She received a terrific evaluation on that trial run, and I started placing her regularly. Gloria had a great attitude and expressed a strong desire to learn. I had a feeling that she wouldn't be a receptionist for long."

Six months after she started temping, Gloria was assigned to a children's theatrical agency. "I just loved the people there," Gloria remembers, and she was fascinated by that kind of work. "I always loved show business, but I never dreamed that I would ever wind up making my living in that world."

Gloria was originally sent to the agency on a two-week assignment, but she was eventually requested back for an indefinite period.

"As time went on," Gloria recalls, "I started getting a feel for the business. One of my neighbors had a little girl that I thought would be perfect for commercials. I referred her to the agency, and my neighbor's daughter soon landed several national TV spots.

"After that, the president of the company asked if I'd be interested in training to be a full-time agent. I was absolutely thrilled, but I told him I couldn't make a definite commitment until I discussed the offer with my personnel coordinator. Joyce said she was very happy for me and that she was certain that the service would be able to work out something equitable with my new employers."

Within five years, Gloria had established herself as a leading agent in her field. Her clients work in movies, national commercials and on top TV shows. Gloria and her two children recently moved into a new house, and they are living better now than ever before.

"I owe a tremendous debt of gratitude to Joyce and the other people at my service," says Gloria. "I would never have even thought of pursuing this kind of career had it not been for temping.

"As far as my marriage is concerned, I guess it was destined to end one way or the other. Any man capable of walking out on his family isn't someone you want to share a life with. Naturally, the children still have some problems about their father deserting them. Still, in the long run, I honestly feel that we're all better off.

"Do I ever think of tracking my ex down and getting

even with him? To be honest, the thought sometimes does cross my mind. But, as the saying goes: Living well is the best revenge."

Gloria is a wonderful example of someone who was able to take a crisis situation and use it as the foundation for building a more self-fulfilling life. We derive a great deal of pleasure in helping people like Gloria rebuild their lives. Our satisfaction is boundless when we are credited in assisting such individuals to unearth talents and achieve goals that even they never envisioned.

▮ *Putting Out the Welcome Mat*

We've mentioned Uniforce's *Get Up and Go* program with respect to people who, for one reason or another, travel from city to city. Like most major services, we use our network of offices to provide a touchstone for people in this increasingly mobile society. Wherever our people go, they feel good knowing that the welcome mat will be waiting for them.

Our *Get Up and Go* program addresses many needs. Perhaps one or more of them may be relevant to you—either now or in the future. Some of you may know in advance that you will be in another city for a period of time and want to ensure that you will have a way to earn extra money. Others may have a spouse who is being relocated to a new job and wish to hit the ground running in terms of generating income and making new contacts.

Perhaps you are someone who likes to travel as part of a workstyle that puts a strong emphasis on leisure. In our business, we are meeting more and more people who prefer this kind of balance in their lives. We know all too well, however, that not all travel decisions are quite so discretionary. When people lose their jobs, they sometimes feel pressed to try their luck in another geographical area. This is yet another circumstance where temporary services can be of help.

When Reuben was laid off his job working for the state of New York, he and his wife Caryn decided to take their two children and move to Florida. The family had very little in the way of savings. Then the transmission on their Toyota died on the second day of the trip. The resulting $1,200 repair bill depleted a significant portion of their funds.

Upon arriving in Florida, Reuben and Caryn rented a two-bedroom apartment. After paying the first and last month's rent and installing a telephone, they found their finances almost totally exhausted. Reuben had originally estimated that he could find work within a month. But now the family was facing an immediate cash crunch.

Fortunately, Caryn had done some temporary secretarial work for a service in New York that had offices nationwide. When she called her personnel coordinator in that office and explained her predicament, Caryn received a promise that her records would be forwarded to Florida within 24 hours.

The next day, Caryn arrived at the Florida office and was pleased to find that her file had, indeed, arrived. As it happened, there were a number of assignments available for someone with Caryn's qualifications, and she was able to start working that same afternoon.

Naturally, Caryn and her husband were relieved that money would soon be coming in. However, this new situation required some logistical changes in the family's plans. Reuben agreed to watch the children for the first month while Caryn earned enough money to give the family a bit of breathing room. After that, Caryn would work fewer hours while Reuben looked for a job.

It took Reuben almost two months to find work, but much of the pressure was alleviated due to the income generated by Caryn. During that time, Caryn had learned Microsoft Word for Windows, an in-demand word processing program. After Reuben started working, Caryn requested and received a three-evening-a-week word processing assignment.

The family's aggregate income is now greater than it was before Reuben lost his job. Both parents are sharing in putting bread on the table and caring for the children. They are all very happy living in Florida.

"Frankly, I don't know what would have happened to us if it weren't for temping," Caryn admits. "We were almost completely broke, and I can't think of any other way that we would have been able to generate income so quickly. Things have really turned out well. We love our new home and our new lifestyle.

"I enjoy word processing work so much I'd like to add more hours to my work schedule. I've also made some good friends on my various temping assignments. That's very important, because we had no social contacts when we arrived. As I told my personnel coordinator, temping has helped me pay my bills, learn a great new skill and put me in places where I could meet new people."

Caryn's previous temping experience certainly worked in her favor. But even if you've never been affiliated with a temporary service, you can walk into a service in any city, and have a reasonably good chance of landing an assignment.

If you have a resumé and documentation establishing your work history, make sure to bring it with you. If you can take skill evaluations the day you have your temporary service interview, so much the better. The more information and documentation you can provide, the faster a service will be able to help you.

If at all possible, we strongly recommend that you sign up with a service that maintains a national network of offices *before* you move. By letting your service know your itinerary in advance, you can avoid finding yourself stranded and broke in a strange city. Taking this step in advance of a move will enable you to take advantage of *Get Up and Go* and similar programs that in effect plug you into a national network of money-making opportunities and social contacts.

As we stated earlier, a crisis does not necessarily mean

that something horrible is going on in your life. Remember, one of the definitions for the word crisis is a turning point. There are all sorts of things that can precipitate turning points in a person's life. When that happens, you might find yourself in need of money, human companionship, or even a place to go for a certain number of hours each day.

Obviously, temporary employment is not the answer to every crisis or turning point a person may face in life. It has, however, proven to be a particularly useful solution for people who find themselves in the following situations:

Needed—Money for College

Just as job security can no longer be guaranteed, neither can a college education be considered an entitlement. We talked earlier about the need to become independent and to assume responsibility for our own well-being. A growing number of college students are now being forced to develop these strengths at a young age.

The costs of tuition, books and living expenses have escalated dramatically, even in state and city colleges. Consequently, more and more college students must generate an income in order to defray these costs. Temping offers young people in such circumstances a way to earn money as well as develop critical skills that can prove to be as important as a college degree.

Susan didn't know how she was going to make it through her sophomore year of college until a friend introduced her to temping. Even with a government loan and some help from her parents, Susan could not cover her costs and expenses.

Susan's personnel coordinator helped her customize a plan that would enable her to work while carrying a reduced class load. Although it will take her six years to graduate instead of four, Susan feels that the tradeoff is worthwhile.

"By the time I receive my degree," notes Susan, "I'll

have a good deal of work experience under my belt. I expect this to make me more marketable to potential employers."

 ## Wanted—A Way to Reenter the Work Force

People who have been out of the job market for a period of time face an important transition when they decide to return. Such women and men often feel out of touch with the work routine or fear that they are ill equipped in terms of possessing up-to-date skills.

Those returning to the world of work after an extended absence find temping ideal for brushing up on existing skills and learning new ones. Many services are now equipped to ease this transition by offering a wide range of training and cross-training opportunities. Temping also provides a comfortable stepping-stone that allows people to ease themselves into the right workstyle niche. And, as we have seen, that niche sometimes turns out to be a career in temporary employment.

There are an estimated 14 million nonworking women caring for their families at home and over 3 million men and women who have taken early retirement.[12] Members of these two large groups are filling an increasing number of jobs that will continue to become available into the twenty-first century. Temping offers a most practical and comfortable way for these individuals to enter or reenter the work force.

 ## The New Emancipated Woman

A growing number of women who have dedicated themselves to caring for their families now find that their children have reached the point where they no longer require full-time care. Nancy is typical of so-called "baby boom mothers" whose children are now grown or almost grown.

"I received my college degree in the late 1960's, when I was in my twenties," Nancy recalls. "I then proceeded to devote more than 20 years to raising my three children. My eldest son is now enrolled in a Ph.D. program; my daughter is a sophomore in college. Neither of them lives at home any longer. My other son is a high school junior who is active in various after-school sports programs.

"About a year ago it occurred to me that there was no real reason for me to continue being a full-time homemaker. In the past I'd been active in scouts and various parents organizations. But these things were no longer demanding my attention.

"My husband and I were managing quite well financially, so there was no pressing need for me to work. On the other hand, some extra money coming in is always welcome when you've got two kids in college and one knocking on the door. More importantly, though, I felt that it was time to pick up that part of my life that I set aside when I chose to devote myself to raising a family.

"I spoke to the principal of my son's high school, and asked if any teaching positions were available. He said there was nothing at present and indicated that it was unlikely that there would be any openings in the near future. The school secretary, whom I had known for years, happened to overhear part of my conversation with the principal. She pulled me aside and suggested that I contact a local temporary service that had placed several of her friends.

"The person who interviewed me at the service was very helpful. She understood that I was experiencing a difficult transition in my life. I always figured that I would be able to teach should the need or desire arise. But I had absolutely no experience in the kind of office positions she had available.

"What if we start you out as a customer service representative in a local bank?" she asked. "You are well spoken and have a pleasant personality. I think this assignment might prove to be a good fit."

Nancy enjoyed the personal contact that customer service work provided. Since she wanted to sample different kinds of work environments, her personnel coordinator placed her in a variety of receptionist, data entry and telemarketing positions. In each case, Nancy received rave reviews from her job supervisor.

"I'm not yet sure where all of this is going to lead," says Nancy. "But I really like the office environment far more than I anticipated. I plan to register for a word processing course at my local community college. I find the idea of working on computers challenging. Also, I've heard that these skills often enable capable women to move up the corporate ladder."

Nancy's impression is right on the money. The 66 million women who will populate corporate America by the year 2000 will fill positions on every rung of the ladder. Many of these will be baby boomers who are entering or reentering the work force. As Patricia Aburdene and John Naisbitt note in *Megatrends for Women:*

"Baby boom women, dedicated to the memory of the youth culture their generation created, will break every stereotype of the postmenopausal woman . . . Freed up from family responsibilities, revered for (their) knowledge and experience . . . they will be treasured as a great human resource."[13]

Temporary services have been leaders in recognizing this trend and embracing homemakers who seek to bring their considerable talents into the workplace. While opportunities exist in a wide range of fields, the automated office is perhaps the most fertile area for women who wish to enter and move up the corporate ladder.

According to the authors of *Megatrends for Women,* America will need 250,000 new secretaries as well as 158,000 medical and 133,000 legal secretaries by the year 2005. For women who are willing to learn word processing, secretarial work offers great opportunity.

Those, like Nancy, who have both a college education and extensive life experience have the best chance of using this skill as a means of establishing a foothold on the ladder of success. It is important to note, however, that many women who do not possess college degrees have also used secretarial skills as a stepping-stone to more prestigious positions.

There is still a sense, in some quarters, that a secretary is another of those traditional "women's jobs" that exist to perform caretaking functions for male bosses. For this reason, many secretaries prefer titles like *executive assistant or administrative assistant.* Whatever you call such positions, though, secretaries are no longer taking a backseat in terms of compensation. They are, in fact, the backbone and mainstay of many successful businesses.

According to a study by *Nine-to-Five,* an association of office workers, a top secretary can earn as much as $75,000 per year in New York City and $50,000 in other major cities. Secretaries who work directly for top corporate executives are well respected, often wield considerable power and can earn salaries that come close to the six-figure range.[14]

▮ *Gray Is Great*

One of the most profound transitions in life is actually a process which affects us all. Aging is a phenomenon that should be seen as one of growth and experience. Unfortunately, it frequently takes on a negative connotation in our youth-obsessed culture.

Too often, older people are viewed as being less productive contributors on the job. We in the temporary services industry realize that nothing can be further from the truth. At Uniforce we embrace older workers. In fact, we have set up a program that offers special benefits to retirees who embrace the temp workstyle.

In case you're someone who has not even begun to think about retirement, it might interest you to know that workers between the ages of forty to seventy are legally defined as "older" under the Age Discrimination in Employment Act. This is an interesting statistic, if you consider that baby boomers now comprise over a third of our population. By the turn of the century, virtually all of these men and women will be over forty. Many will have passed their fiftieth birthday.[15]

It is ironic that the majority of men and women whose generation coined the term *youth culture* are now classified as "older." Not to worry. There's still time before those of you in that group reach the magic age of 55—the year, it seems, when the gradual transition of aging reaches what many consider to be a tangible turning point.

Why, you may wonder, should 55 be viewed as a chronological milestone? After all, most people are still vital and productive well beyond that age. Part of the answer lies in a growing trend in corporate America to induce people to accept early retirement. According to economist Pat Choate, these often generous inducements to retire are motivated by two primary considerations:

1. To make room for younger, unvested and lower paid people who are thought to be more aggressive and more capable.

2. To reduce salaries, benefits and pensions—costs that tend to increase as an employee attains greater seniority.[16]

It is becoming a fairly common practice for someone to take early retirement, only to be rehired through a temporary service to perform exactly the same functions. The telling difference in the two situations is the savings in benefits which, as we have seen, can add an additional 40 percent or more to an employer's costs.

Although mandatory retirement is now prohibited in most states and for most job categories, the Bureau of Labor Statistics estimates that over 50 percent of all workers retire before age 65. A growing number are accepting early retirement. The vast majority of these people are, in fact, not being forced to vacate their jobs. Nor do most men and women retire because of reduced productivity or poor health.

These are the five answers we most often receive when we ask interviewees why they opted for retirement or early retirement:

1. I felt my opportunities were limited.
2. I was unhappy with my work environment.
3. I no longer found my work satisfying.
4. My employer convinced me to accept early retirement.
5. I wanted more leisure time.

Although there are laws prohibiting age discrimination, it is impossible to legislate against the prejudicial ways some people feel. Despite evidence to the contrary, too many employers continue to believe that older workers are less productive, less able to learn new skills and more likely to quit work than younger employers. However, as Pat Choate points out: "These biases are self-fulfilling. There is much evidence that older workers are at least as productive as their younger counterparts, and even more so in some occupations."[17]

To back up this contention, Choate cites the following statistics:

-   According to the U.S. Department of Labor, worker productivity declines only slightly after age 45, and then a bit more after age 65.

-   Clerks and typists are among those occupations in which the accuracy and reliability of workers aged 65 and over are as good or better than that of their younger counterparts.

-   In a study conducted by The American Council of Life Insurance, workers over 45 were found to lose fewer days to sickness than younger workers.

-   A study by *Nine-to-Five*, an association of office workers, found turnover rates among older women to be nearly 90 percent lower than those of younger women.

The above data confirm something that we in the temporary services industry have understood for many years. Aside from being illegal, age-based discrimination has no foundation in fact. Furthermore, it results in substantial losses of productivity among older Americans—losses that impact negatively upon us all.

We have found that, despite the prevailing stereotypes, older workers value their jobs and are often more stable and responsible than their younger colleagues. That's why we value people in the 55-and-over age range. The temporary industry has tremendous opportunities for older workers who want to supplement their retirement income and set their own workstyle and lifestyle schedules.

Temporary services do not discriminate on the basis of age. In fact, most services welcome the experience, knowledge and ability of older workers. The industry is proud to have emerged as one of the nation's largest employers of people in the 55-and-over age bracket, and we intend to continue maintaining that position in the future.

For those of you who have already retired, we urge you to cherish this time in your life as a golden opportunity to do some of those things you put off when you worked full time. We are aware, however, that many of you feel that you would like to continue working. If so, we invite you to join us. Temping is the best way we know to have a second career without undertaking the kind of long-term commitment most permanent jobs require.

The professionals at your temporary service will be glad to help you customize a plan that meets your needs. If you wish, they will show you how to work just enough to supplement your income without jeopardizing your social security and other benefits.

Aside from enabling you to generate extra income, temping provides a perfect opportunity to meet new people, learn new skills and remain a vital and productive contributor. These advantages come without the stresses that may have accompanied the permanent jobs you had in the past.

Should you wish to travel or take time off to visit friends and family, that's fine. Temporary services specialize in helping people create flexible workstyle schedules that are custom tailored to their lifestyle needs.

Some retirees have the psychic makeup and financial freedom to stop working completely. These men and women are able to enjoy endless days of leisure and are glad to be free of work. On the other hand, we've seen too many older people experience a loss of direction and self-esteem once they retire. After years of having a place to go and a structured schedule, they feel that their lives lack shape and purpose.

We believe that retirement presents an opportunity to reinvent yourself. If you want or need to work, temporary services are uniquely equipped to help you find the workstyle that is best suited to your lifestyle requirements. We welcome the opportunity to prove to you that your age is an asset—not a barrier—in the workplace, and in life!

▌ Notes

1. Carolyn Corbin, *The Lifeskills Lecture Series*, (Dallas, TX: Carolyn Corbin, Inc. 1992).

2. *The Random House College Dictionary*, (New York: Random House, 1990).

3. Howard Putnam, *The Winds of Turbulence: A CEO's Reflections on Surviving and Thriving on the Cutting Edge of Corporate Crisis*, (New York: Harper Business, 1991).

4. *The New York Times*, May 12, 1992.

5. Bruce Springsteen, "My Hometown," *Born in the U.S.A.*, Columbia Records (1984).

6. Carolyn Corbin, *Strategies 2000,* (Austin, TX: Eakin Press, 1991 revised edition).

7. Corbin, *Lifeskills.*

8. Bernard Rothman, *Loving & Leaving: Winning at the Business of Divorce,* (Lexington, MA: Lexington Books, 1991).

9. *Ibid.*

10. 1990 U.S. Census Bureau Statistics.

11. Rothman.

12. John Naisbitt and Patricia Aburdene, *Megatrends 2000,* (New York: William Morrow, 1990).

13. Patricia Aburdene and John Naisbitt, *Megatrends for Women,* (New York: Villard Books, 1992).

14. *Nine to Five,* as cited in *Megatrends for Women.*

15. 1990 U.S. Census Bureau Statistics.

16. Pat Choate and J. K. Linger, *High-Flex Society: Shaping America's Economic Future,* (New York: Alfred A. Knopf, 1986).

17. *Ibid.*

10

Create Your Personalized Temporary Employment Game Plan

Now that you have an overview of the workstyle opportunities temporary services provide, we want to work with you in structuring a personalized game plan.

We respect the fact that each of you has your own unique needs and priorities. In that sense, no category can adequately depict who you are. Nevertheless, we have come to recognize certain common denominators among women and men who seek temporary employment. These are expressed in the following descriptive groupings:

- Working mothers in two-income families
- People between jobs

- Empty nesters
- Students
- Recent college graduates
- Retirees and early retirees
- Moonlighters
- Creative and performing artists
- Free spirits

Later in this chapter we will look at some time-management issues that are critical in formulating your own personal plan of action. But first, we'd like to share some guidelines that have proven helpful to people seeking to design workstyles that are best suited to each of the following lifestyles:

▌ *Working Mothers in Two-Income Families*

These women tend to be most concerned with achieving the kind of balanced lifestyle that was discussed in Chapter Seven. Oftentimes, their children are in school for the better part of the day. Consequently, an important objective is to be present during those hours when the children are home.

Some working mothers must have specific days of the week off so that they can fulfill car-pooling responsibilities, take their children to after-school activities or attend teacher conferences or doctor's appointments. Temporary services are geared to accommodate such lifestyle considerations.

Other mothers who want or need to work have pre-school children who demand more of their time. Parents who need to be home all day with their children can seek evening and weekend assignments in such fields as word processing, retailing, telemarketing or data-entry work. This type of scheduling works out well for couples who want to share childcare and income-generating responsibilities.

We work with many families in which the wife leaves for her temporary assignment shortly after the husband gets home from his full-time job. Sometimes, when the two schedules can't be coordinated quite so precisely, a baby-sitter may have to be hired to fill in between the time Mom leaves for work and Dad arrives home.

A second possibility for a working mother with home responsibilities is to take a long-term, temporary assignment and share it with another mother. In such a job-sharing arrangement, Jane might work two days in a given week, while Margaret works three days. On alternate weeks the two might switch schedules: Jane would work three days and Margaret two days. Two mothers who agree to such an arrangement can also share baby-sitting duties.

If this kind of time-sharing arrangement interests you and you lack a partner, ask your temporary service if it can find someone for you. Since a large percentage of the temp work force are homemakers, such requests are often able to be accommodated. Whatever your specific requirements, the temporary workstyle provides many alternatives for today's working mother. In considering temping, working mothers should follow a game plan, such as:

GAME PLAN FOR WORKING MOTHERS

- Let your service know exactly when you want to work.

- Give specific dates of summer and other school vacations when you may not be available.

- Be careful not to accept assignments that extend into the above dates.

- If your scheduling requirements change frequently, do not request or accept lengthy assignments. Tell your personnel coordinator that you prefer week-to-week assignments so that your availability for the following week can be assessed.

▌ *People Between Jobs*

When you are out of work, it is important to seek temporary assignments that afford you the opportunity to showcase your skills to potential employers. Try to become affiliated with services that have assignments in industries where your background and experience lie. If possible, try to ascertain in advance whether the service can send you to companies where you want to be employed. Depending on your professional skills, you may want to register with a general and/or specialty service.

As we discussed in Chapter Eight, it is important to let your service know in advance that you are looking for a permanent position. In addition to signing up with one or more temporary services, you may also want to register with a personnel agency that specializes in securing full-time positions in your field.

Should one or more job prospects be in the wind, you may need to take some time off to follow up and attend interviews. For this reason, it may be best not to accept long-term assignments. In any case, if you apprise your personnel coordinator of your plans and objectives, she will work with you in formulating the most appropriate game plan.

It's important to remember that temporary services are themselves good sources of leads for companies that are hiring for permanent positions. Furthermore, the assignments on which they send you can often result in permanent job offers. In a survey of 300 personnel administrators, 63 percent of the respondents reported that they sometimes promote or hire temps for full-time, permanent employment.[1]

Even if a permanent job offer does not materialize from your temporary assignments, your service can still be instrumental in helping you achieve your career objectives. By keeping you working, temporary services make it possible to show continuity on your resumé. If you make it a point to perform well and maintain a positive attitude on all your temporary assignments, your service can be an excellent job-reference source. That's why it's in your interest to think of temporary services in the same light as other employers. People between jobs should have a game plan:

GAME PLAN FOR JOB HUNTERS

- Seek opportunities to showcase your skills and talents.
- Affiliate yourself with services that specialize in your field.
- Let your personnel coordinator know that you are interested in temp-to-perm opportunities.
- Consider registering with a permanent personnel agency that specializes in full-time work in your field.
- Make sure you have an attractive, up-to-date resumé that sells you to potential employers. Your resumé should be professionally typed or printed on high quality paper. Its length should be no more than two pages.
- Find out about each company to which you are applying so that you can write customized cover letters.
- Prepare a reference sheet. If you are stating that references will be furnished upon request, be sure to have them ready. Paper and type style should match your resumé. Make sure to let your references know that people may be calling.
- Design a temporary workstyle that allows taking time off for job hunting and interviews.
- Remember, your service is a potentially valuable source of contacts and references, so act accordingly.
- Network among friends, former employers and business associates. Let everyone know that you are job hunting.

▉ *Empty Nesters*

If you are considering a return to the work force after a long period of caring for your family, temping can be an especially attractive alternative. Temp services recognize and value the life skills you bring to a job. As was discussed in Chapters Two and Nine, one of the things a temporary service does best is helping people in transitional situations.

Some of our reentry women use temping as a stepping-stone to a permanent position. Others eventually decide that career temping is their best option. Whichever path you eventually choose, temporary employment is especially well suited to people in your position.

When you walk into the office of an established service, expect to be warmly received. Don't worry about how long you've been out of the workplace. As we've noted earlier: *Temporary services are looking to screen you in—not out!*

One of the first things services will do is help you assess your skills—free of charge. Afterwards, they will talk to you about the most appropriate way to ease you back into the work force.

Most general-assignment services have opportunities at all levels. Therefore, if your skills are rusty or you need time to develop new skills, your personnel coordinator will place you in an entry-level assignment. As we noted in Chapter Three, there are many receptionist and light clerical positions available.

While the remuneration for such assignments may not be at the top of the scale, such positions do provide a good way for reentry people to build confidence and upgrade their skills. We know hundreds of women who started temping on this level and within a matter of a few months worked their way into more interesting and higher paying positions. Temping gives you an opportunity to do just that—and at your own pace.

Perhaps you possess job skills that you haven't used for some time. If so, temping will give you an opportunity to regain and update those skills. Throughout these pages we've seen a number of instances where people who could type were able to acquire in-demand word processing skills in a relatively short time period. There are self-tutorials that enable you to train yourself just by arranging practice time on a computer or dedicated word processor. We've also presented examples of women who were able to use temping as a way to turn their life skills into rewarding career opportunities.

Whether you want to resume your former career or start anew, a good temporary service will be able to place you on assignments that are appropriate for your skill level and on which you will feel comfortable. In either case, if you've been out of the workplace for a number of years, you may find jumping right into a full-time work schedule a bit too demanding. Fortunately, temporary services usually have an inventory of two- or three-day-a-week assignments from which you can choose.

When you sit down with a professional temporary service assignment coordinator, she will help you determine the most appropriate number of days for you to work and the kind of work environment where you will feel most comfortable. Reentry women can use the following game plan:

GAME PLAN FOR REENTRY WOMEN

- Proceed with confidence. Even if you've been out of the job market for a number of years, your experience as a homemaker has given you some important organizational and management skills. These will be very valuable in any job situation.

- When you go for your temporary service interview, be sure to mention any skills, previous organizational or fund-raising experience that might be relevant to a job situation.

- Think about the other factors in your life, and decide the number of days that you will be comfortable working.

Start off slowly, perhaps with a two- or three-day-per-week assignment, and increase at a comfortable pace.

- Choose a service that offers training and cross-training opportunities that are of interest to you.

- Set achievable goals so that you can build self-esteem and success experiences as you progress.

 ## *Students*

Young people who are attending college have long used temping to earn money for tuition and other expenses. As these costs escalate, we find that more and more students are taking advantage of this option. Aside from helping generate money, temping offers students excellent opportunities to build their resumés and gain the kind of practical work experience that makes job hunting after graduation a far less intimidating and mysterious process.

As we discussed in Chapters Eight and Nine, experiences garnered in the workplace tend to be more highly regarded than the ones students receive in a classroom. Many of our clients tell us that they value a good on-the-job performance rating more highly than an A in the classroom.

Temping provides the kind of real-world experience you just can't get in school. If you have a special interest in a particular field or profession, let your service know, and it will try to place you accordingly.

When Seth was a college freshman, his goal was to become an attorney. Upon registering with his local temporary service, Seth asked his personnel coordinator if she could assign him to a job at a law firm. While she was unable to fill this request immediately, Seth's personnel coordinator was eventually able to place him as an in-house messenger at a large corporate law firm. Because Seth's supervisor was pleased with his work, he was assigned to the firm during much of his college career.

After his first year of law school, Seth was offered an

assignment as a clerk. Upon passing the bar, he was rewarded with an associate attorney's position. During the time Seth worked as a messenger, the partners got to know and like him. By the time he graduated law school, Seth had proven his worth and understood the workings of the company.

In a society where apprenticeships and internships are becoming exceedingly rare, temporary services have been taking up the slack. Whether you work throughout the school year—or just during summers or vacations, temping gives you a unique opportunity to earn extra money, gain critical work experience and make valuable contacts. Students can use the following game plan:

GAME PLAN FOR STUDENTS

- Assess your financial needs vs. the time you need to complete your schoolwork successfully.

- Even if you don't need extra money, consider temping during summers and/or vacations as a way to build your resumé.

- Apprise your personnel coordinator of your short- and long-range goals.

- In filling out your work-history card, be sure to include any clubs, teams, volunteer work or affiliations. These enhance your resumé and demonstrate stability and commitment.

- Try to project a professional attitude and demeanor. This is a particularly desirable quality for any young person to possess.

- If you have an interest in a particular field or career, ask your personnel coordinator to assign you to relevant companies.

- Try to acquire at least one in-demand skill, such as word processing. A relatively short course can make you eligible for a higher pay rate and expose you to a wider range of opportunities.

▌ *Recent College Graduates*

As we saw in Chapter Eight, many college graduates are having a difficult time finding suitable employment. Temping is truly a beacon of light in this kind of depressed job market. In a significant number of cases, temporary assignments lead to permanent jobs. And even if that goal isn't achieved, temping provides you with a way to earn money while you are conducting your job search.

If you are among those college graduates who possess personal computer skills, a service should be able to provide a choice of attractive assignments. Again, it is important to let your personnel coordinator know that you want a permanent position. This will enable her to put you on a temp-to-perm track, and to factor in your potential need to take time off to job hunt.

It is generally accepted that finding a job is easier when you already have a job. To a great extent that's true. However, once you do secure a permanent position, there won't be a lot of time to go looking for something better. That's why we want to urge you to think twice before accepting any position that does not correspond to your long-range objectives.

As we see it, temping is the best way to maximize your options while you're in the process of looking for a permanent job. It fills the immediate need of providing income, while giving you an opportunity to sample different companies and corporate cultures. In addition, temping makes it possible for you to structure a schedule that allows as much time as you need to pursue promising situations that you might generate on your own or through a personnel agency. Recent college grads can use the following game plan:

GAME PLAN FOR RECENT COLLEGE GRADUATES

- Register with a service that can assign you to companies where you have an interest in working.

- Let your personnel coordinator know that you have temp-to-perm aspirations.

- Consider also signing up with a permanent personnel agency that specializes in job opportunities in your area.

- Create a work schedule that allows sufficient time for job hunting.

- If possible, try not to jump at the first permanent job offer if it doesn't seem right for you. Before you take the plunge, try first to test the waters by temping at each company you may be considering.

- Make the most of each temporary assignment by using it as an opportunity to develop contacts and build your resumé.

▮ *Retirees and Early Retirees*

As we discussed in Chapters Two and Nine, the temporary workstyle is a particularly good choice for retirees of all ages. Men and women who have worked hard for many years welcome the opportunity to travel and spend time pursuing a variety of leisure and creative activities. At the same time, a growing number of retirees want or need to continue working. Temping is a great way to achieve the exact balance that's right for you.

If you find that your social security and pension benefits do not enable you to live at the level you desire, the temporary workstyle makes it possible to keep working without jeopardizing those entitlements. Once your personnel coordinator is aware of your financial parameters and lifestyle needs, she will help you design the perfect plan for you.

There are a growing number of retirees who are glad that they no longer have to deal with the stress of a high pressure job. At the same time, they are nowhere near ready for that proverbial rocking chair. Temporary services have a wide variety of assignments for retirees. Best of all: you can work as many days as you wish and for as long as you wish.

Do you want to work a five-day week for two months and then travel for the next six months? No problem. Do you want to work three days per week for this month and two days a week next month? Just keep your personnel coordinator apprised of your needs, and she will help customize the best workstyle plan for you.

Naturally, the time you put in on the job is only one of several considerations. If you're like many of the retirees we know, you're looking for a comfortable work environment that is challenging but not stressful. Temporary service professionals are sensitive to these feelings and are committed to helping you succeed.

Are you now retired and thinking about returning to the work force? If so, temporary employment can give you a second career opportunity. Some retirees may feel that one career is quite enough, and we certainly respect that. If, however, you want to generate additional income, learn new skills, meet new people and continue leading a productive and useful life, temping is an option you owe it to yourself to consider.

As we noted earlier, many services have instituted special programs for retirees. At many Uniforce offices, retirees automatically receive a free membership in the American Association of Retired Persons (AARP), as well as a variety of discounts, benefits and bonuses.

We sincerely believe that working as a temp in a second career can be more pleasurable and rewarding than the career you had before retiring. In fact, our retired people have a motto that expresses just how pleased they are with the temporary workstyle: *Work is lovelier the second time around.*

If you or someone you know is retired or planning to retire in the near future, we invite you to come in for a second-career consultation at your earliest convenience. At most major services, these consultations are free. And, of course, there is never a fee when a service sends you out on assignment. Retirees can use the following game plan:

GAME PLAN FOR RETIREES AND EARLY RETIREES

- If you were induced to take early retirement and want to continue working, see if your company is interested in retaining you through a temporary service. The service simply transfers you to the service's payroll. At that point, your company will decide whether you will retain medical and other benefits or be paid on an hourly basis. If you so desire, a service might also be able to secure a similar position for you at a different company.

- If you are interested in a second career, take appropriate skill evaluations and let your personnel coordinator know about any other skills, talents and relevant work and/or life experience you might possess.

- Sit down with your personnel coordinator and evaluate your short- and long-term financial situation. This will help you determine how much you need to work to sustain your lifestyle needs.

- Make sure you are aware of the amount of money you are legally permitted to earn without endangering your social security, pension and other retirement benefits.

- Take advantage of appropriate training and cross-training opportunities offered by your service.

- Factor in your desire to travel and pursue other activities when working out your schedule. Always keep your personnel coordinator apprised of any changes.

- Network with other retirees by joining AARP and similar organizations.

- Help your service place you on assignments where you will feel happy. Maintain a dialogue with your personnel coordinator. Even if you are able to accept a long-term assignment, don't feel you have to jump at the first offer. Wait until you find a situation in which you sense you will be happy.

- Don't sell yourself short. No matter what your age or skill level, most temporary services can place retirees who have a good work ethic and a positive attitude. Similarly, a long absence from the workplace should not present a problem. If you have a genuine desire to work, the fastest way to achieve that goal is to contact a temporary-service professional.

▌ Moonlighters

People who need second jobs during evening or weekend hours in order to generate additional income are well served by the temporary workstyle option. Weekend, evening, second- and third-shift opportunities exist in a large number of marketplaces.

If you work a conventional 9-to-5 job, temporary services can provide assignments in fields ranging from computer programming and operations to word processing, telemarketing, data entry and light assembly work. Men and women are often needed to fill these positions on night and weekend shifts.

There are also a multitude of evening and weekend assignments available in the medical field. Home health aides, licensed practical nurses, registered nurses and clerical hospital staff are often in great demand. As was noted in Chapter Three, this is one of the fastest growing areas in temporary employment.

If you are interested in hospitality assignments, there are numerous opportunities in catering, fast food, hotels and restaurants. Most temp services supply staff to those business sources. Whatever your field of interest or expertise, temporary services are skilled at addressing the concerns of men and women who need to supplement their income.

Members of the teaching profession are one group who

are attracted to the moonlighting opportunities offered by temping. Teachers generally have summers off and work a 200-day year. Temporary employment enables them to supplement their income by doing work that is very different from that in the classroom.

At most large services you'll find teachers who work as—among other things—word processors, bookkeepers, telemarketers and customer service representatives. These professionals often enjoy sampling a variety of work environments. They especially like the flexibility of being able to work only when the need or desire arises. Moonlighters can use the following game plan:

GAME PLAN FOR MOONLIGHTERS

- Assess your need for extra money vs. your availability to take on additional work.

- As much as possible, try to find assignments at your highest skill level.

- Make sure you sign up with a service that has a choice of assignments that are right for you.

- Don't accept assignments that will hinder your performance on your regular job.

- In order to keep motivated and avoid boredom, consider asking for temporary assignments that are different from the kind of work you regularly do.

▉ *Creative and Performing Artists*

As we discussed in Chapter Two, people who seek to establish themselves in artistic careers must often do some other kind of work to pay the bills. Such men and women are often caught in a quandary: They need to devote a good deal of time to their creative pursuits if they are to have any chance of being recognized and remunerated for their efforts. At the same time, there are pragmatic issues such as paying the rent, buying groceries and the like that must be addressed.

Unless one is independently wealthy or the recipient of a large trust fund, there is no way of avoiding the practical realities of survival. Temporary employment is ideally suited for creators and performers because it provides virtually unlimited flexibility. Let's look at two cases in point:

Doug is a novelist who often works four nights a week as a word processor. His personnel coordinator is aware, however, that Doug needs to take a few weeks off to concentrate on his writing from time to time. Recently, one of his novels was published, and Doug took two months off to do some promotion and public speaking. Afterwards, he returned to temping and is again word processing four nights a week.

Because Doug always lets his personnel coordinator know of his plans well in advance, she is able to accommodate his variable time considerations. Doug hopes one day to make enough money as a novelist to be able to do that full-time. However, as Doug himself recently remarked: "I've been temping for the past seven years. I guess, in some objective sense, you can say that this is my actual career."

Lois is a professional dancer who has performed all over America. Although she is respected in her field, Lois generally doesn't make enough money in most given years to make ends meet. For the past 12 years, Lois has supplemented her income by temping as a receptionist and switchboard operator.

"Temping isn't nearly as glamorous as dancing for a living," Lois admits. "But every month there are bills that need to be paid. If it weren't for my temp service, I don't see how I could continue pursuing dance. As it is, I can accept jobs in different cities because my service has branches all over the country and I am able to temp wherever I might find myself."

Artists can use the following game plan:

GAME PLAN FOR CREATIVE AND PERFORMING ARTISTS

- If possible, try to temp in a field that complements your creative work. For example, actors often do well at telemarketing. Writers frequently have word processing skills.

- Try to temp as much as possible when you are not involved in creative pursuits so that you can build a financial cushion.

- Use your creative flair to design a temporary workstyle that is uniquely yours.

- Keep your personnel coordinator apprised of your schedule. She will do her best to work with you, but she also expects you to be cooperative and respect her needs.

- If you're in the kind of field that requires traveling, try to sign up with one or more services that have a nationwide network of offices.

▌ *Free Spirits*

A growing number of men and women are opting for a freer lifestyle—one that enables them to work when they want while traveling and enjoying life. This group includes men and women in all professions and career fields. You have met—on these pages—secretaries, receptionists, physicians and attorneys who decided that they no longer wanted to be tied down to a permanent job.

Is this free-spirit lifestyle for you? Each individual must make that judgment for her/himself. But, if you should decide to try it out for a while, temporary services are here to turn such adventurous dreams into realities.

Temporary service professionals share the excitement of those free spirits who long for mobility and freedom yet still need or want to work. Our personnel coordinators specialize in creating workstyles to fit a wide variety of life-styles. That means you can work when—as well as where—you want to work. What you do with the rest of the time is your business.

Many of our free spirits love to travel, and we love making that possible. A number of large services now provide a work-travel option. Uniforce's happens to be called the *Get Up and Go* program. Here's how taking advantage of such work-travel plans works:

We realize that some free spirits are not comfortable planning their moves months or even weeks in advance. That won't be a problem as long as you let your service know when you are no longer going to be available for assignments. Then, at some future point, should you find yourself in a new city where your service has an office, you can call and request that your records be sent. Thanks to fax machines and next-day mail services, your file can be expected to arrive in short order. At that point, an appropriate assignment should be forthcoming.

Free spirits can use the following game plan:

GAME PLAN FOR FREE SPIRITS

- Register with one or more temporary services that maintain a national network of offices.

- Always be reliable in dealing with your service. No matter how free your spirit, you are expected to act professionally and tender sufficient notice of any changes in your availability.

- Always try to complete assignments before moving on. If you leave your service in a tight spot, you can hardly expect that it will go out of its way for you.

- Whenever possible, try to let your personnel coordinator know when you will be arriving in a new city, and request that your records be sent ahead.

- Try to maintain a sufficient amount of savings to see you

through times when assignments may not be immediately available.

- When you arrive in a new city on short notice, be prepared to accept a job that does not utilize your most price-worthy talents. Depending on your skills, it may not always be possible for your service to place you at the highest level assignment for which you are qualified—at least not at first.

▌ The Importance of Time Management

No matter what kind of temporary game plan you choose, the way you manage time is an overriding factor that will greatly influence the degree to which you succeed. There are 12 general time management principles that will help ensure your success. We heartily encourage you to take the following into consideration when formulating your temporary employment game plan.

▌ Twelve Time-Saving Tips

1. Establish realistic and specific career objectives. Write down your own job description based on your education, experience, innate talents and personal preferences. Knowing what you want to do will help you get there. This principle can be applied to all areas of your life, including work, personal, family, health and spiritual. Remember the importance of balance. Set aside some quiet time to think about what you would like to accomplish in each of these areas. The balance you come up with is in effect a statement of your personal definition of success.

2. Select the one objective in each of the above areas that is most important. These are your priorities.

3. Spend as much time as possible on your objectives—particularly your priorities.

4. Always work with enthusiasm and energy. Concentrate fully on the matter at hand, even if other things are competing for your attention.

5. Try to always be aware of exactly what you're doing and why.

6. Invest some time maintaining and improving your health. This can ultimately make you more productive and less prone to illness.

7. Pinpoint the most productive times in your day and use them to best advantage.

8. Avoid procrastination by always doing something—no matter how small—to move toward your objectives.

9. Whenever possible, avoid unwanted interruptions and people who sap your energy.

10. When formulating your plans, estimate how long things will take—then add on some additional time.

11. Seek out high-quality leisure activities.

12. Keep your priorities and objectives in mind, even while you're engaged in routine tasks.

We have come to the end of our journey. We hope you found the chapters informative and helpful in formulating your objectives and future plans. We have tried to anticipate your needs and give you as much guidance in those areas as possible. If you have any questions or comments, we would enjoy hearing from you. Please feel free to write us at:

Uniforce Services, Inc.
1335 Jericho Turnpike
New Hyde Park, NY 11040

We'd like to take this opportunity to say that it has been a pleasure spending this time with you. We sincerely hope that you will use what you've learned in this book to take full advantage of the challenge, growth, opportunity and financial rewards that await you in the exciting world of temporary employment.

Here's wishing you the time of your life through temping!

 Notes

1. *Personnel*, August 1988.

Index

Temporary employment:
    career temping, 139-57
    creative/performing artists
        and, 19-21
    crisis/transitional
        temping, 183-209
    disadvantages of, 65-67
    as feeling-out process,
        21-23
    flexibility of, 2, 19-21
    freedom of, 30-32
    and homemakers entering
        the workplace, 23-25
    opportunities in, 40-41
    health-care jobs, 50-53
    industrial jobs, 49-50
    marketing jobs, 47-48
    office jobs, 41-47
    professional temporaries,
        55-60
    technical jobs, 53-54
    as path to permanent
        position, 159-80
    people suited to, 5
    and recently fired/laid off,
        28-29, 59-60
    and retirees, 25-28
    rise in, 40
    as source of second
        income, 17-19
    and transferees, 30
    work style offered by, 1-2
Temporary employment
    industry, 4-5
Temporary-help services, *See*
    Services
Temporary-to-permanent
    position:
    job search, designing, 167
    protocol, 178-80

Test-taking, tips for, 84-86
Time management, 229-31
Transferees:
    crisis/transitional temping
        and, 197-200
    and temporary
        employment, 30
Tuition reimbursement, 136
Turnover costs, temporary
    personnel and, 6

U

Uniforce Services, 2-3, 69, 230
    benefits offered by, 134-36
Careertemp Club, 148
"Get Up & Go" program, 30,
    81, 146, 197
    older workers and, 204-8
"Smart-Hire" program, 167
"You're a Star with Uniforce"
    questionnaire, 128-29
U.S. Department of Labor, 137

V

Vacation pay, 133, 134-35
Value, estimating, 119-21

W

Weekly timecard, 114
Winds of Turbulence, The
    (Putnam), 186
Win-win relationship,
    developing with
    temporary service,
    97-101
Workforce reduction,